Karolina Hołda/Artur Juszczak

Caudron-Renault CR.714 no. 8543, code no. 10 (I-201) of GC 1/145
2nd escadrille, pilot LAC Andrzej Niewiara. Dreux, June 1940.

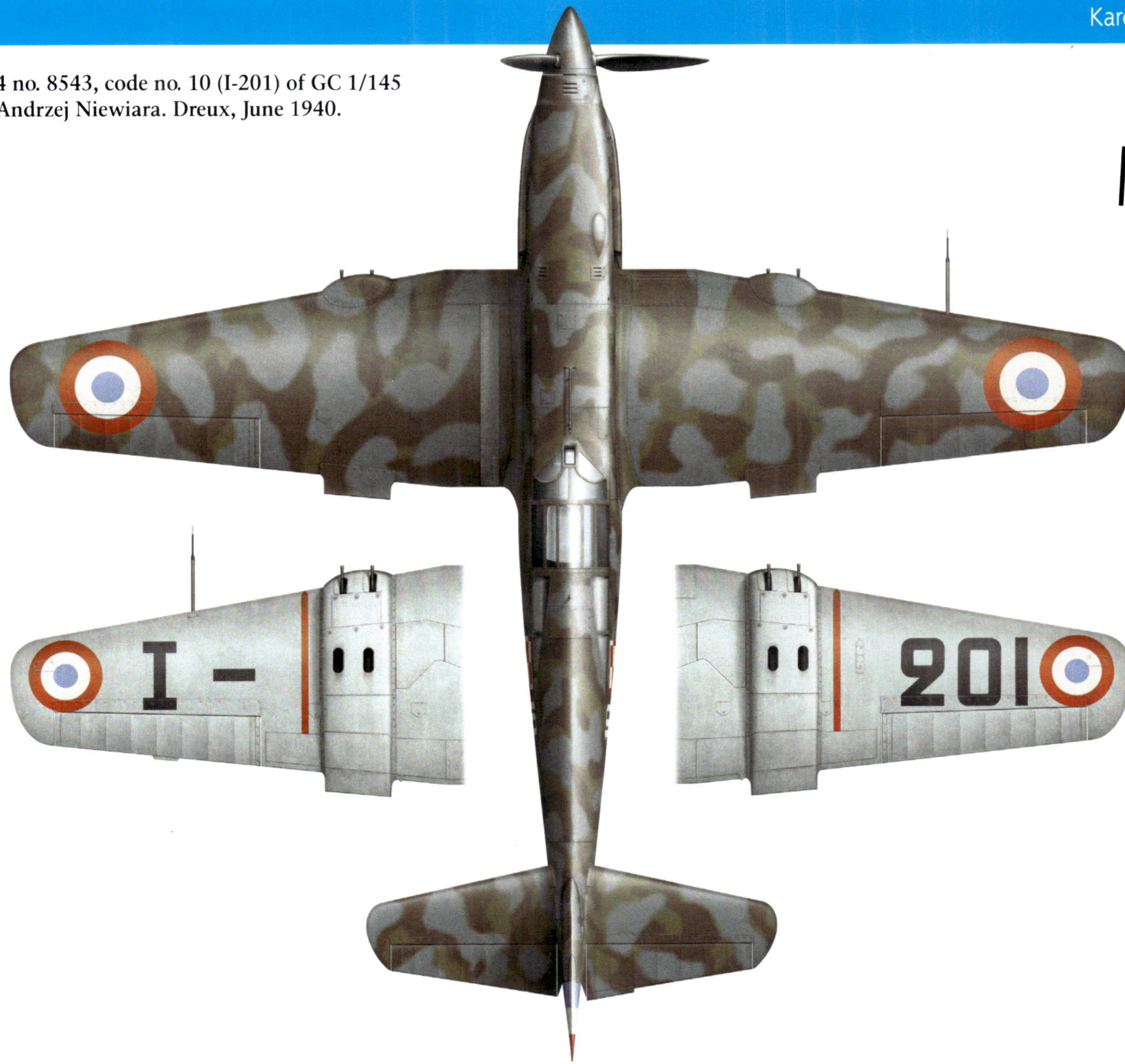

Errata

Fighters over France
1940

STRATUS

Introduction

L'Armee de l'Air in the 1940 Campaign

The "Phoney War" period highlighted to the French High Command the urgent need to modernize the equipment of its fighter units. When France entered the war on 3 September 1939, the French Air Force (Armee de l'Air; AdA) had relatively modern Morane 406s and Curtiss Hawk H-75As in its inventory, equipping 15 fighter squadrons (Groupe de Chasse; GC). However, eight squadrons still relied on outdated aircraft, including the Dewoitine 501/510s, Spad 510s, and Nieuport Delage NiD 622/629s. Additionally, four squadrons operated Potez 631 fighters.

In total, metropolitan airfields housed 472 modern aircraft of varying combat capabilities. Among these, the Curtiss Hawks stood out as the best, with 97 aircraft spread across just four squadrons (GCs I/4, II/4, I/5, and II/5). Despite the lessons that could have been learned from the fall of Poland in 1939, Allied commands failed to adapt effectively. The period of relative calm from October 1939 to May 1940 dulled the vigilance of French military planners.

During this time, some efforts were made to modernize fighter aviation, such as introducing Bloch 151/152 aircraft to front-line units. However, the overall number of fighters available to the AdA remained insufficient. The fighter force was organized into operational zones (Zone des Operations Aeriennes; ZOA), where individual fighter groups (Groupement de Chasse; Grpmt)

Morane MS.406 no 996 of GC III/3 after a force landing on 16 May 1940 in Vertain. It was the personal aircraft of cne. Trouillard, but on that day was piloted by Adj. Chef Morias. (B. Belcarz coll.)

The opening days of the campaign exposed the Allies' lack of preparedness, revealing months of inaction following the fall of Poland. Perhaps they underestimated Hitler, but the German war machine quickly proved otherwise. While the main thrust targeted the Low Countries, no region was safe from German air operations. French units, in particular, suffered heavy losses, often more on the ground than in the air.

German raids on airfields were devastatingly effective. On 10 May 1940, GC III/2 lost 14 Morane 406s in attacks and air combat. A raid on Lagny, the base of GC III/6, on 27 May destroyed 16 MS.406s – over half the unit's inventory. These losses highlighted French negligence in camouflaging aircraft on the ground.

Another factor contributing to German dominance was their superior aircraft guidance system. French interception efforts were often delayed, relying on reports from AA gun crews, rendering responses ineffective. Early French tactics, such as constant air patrols, overstretched resources with little success.

As air superiority slipped away, tactics shifted. Fighter sections from training personnel were formed under the territorial air defense (Défense Aérienne du Territoire, DAT) system to protect specific areas and installations, marking a desperate adjustment to mounting losses.

Phase 2: 27 May – 4 June 1940

This phase bore similarities to the Polish campaign of September 1939, with rapid changes on the ground forcing constant relocation of air force units due to the German blitzkrieg.

Curtis Hawk H-75A captured by German troops. (T. J. Kopański coll.)

Introduction

After Phase 1 ended with the Wehrmacht reaching the Channel and encircling Allied forces at Dunkirk, German air activity briefly subsided. During this lull, the French attempted to regroup, reinforce their units, and adapt their air defense strategy.

With Paris now under direct threat, air units were concentrated around the capital, receiving reinforcements that proved insufficient. To protect key military sites – such as bases, armament factories, and aircraft assembly plants – the **Défense Aérienne du Territoire (DAT)** system was expanded, forming at least 21 sections. These included French (11 sections), Polish (12), Czechoslovak (2), and Belgian (2) pilots. However, DAT units faced significant challenges, including limited resources, lack of an effective airspace monitoring system, and delayed responses to German raids. Most successes were sporadic, achieved by chance encounters during patrols. French pilots in DAT units reportedly downed at least nine enemy aircraft, but overall effectiveness was minimal.

By late May and early June, air operations over France decreased in intensity, as German efforts focused on disrupting Allied evacuations at Dunkirk. Meanwhile, the French Air Force struggled to redeploy and rebuild, but the time available was too short for meaningful recovery. This phase served as a prelude to the fierce battles ahead, particularly in defense of Paris during the Phase 3.

Phase 3: 5–24 June 1940 – German "Operation Paula"

By 5 June 1940, the French Air Force had undergone notable changes in its order of battle. Five units had replaced their Morane 406s with modern Dewoitine D.520s, and GC III/2 had transitioned to Curtiss H-75As after heavy early losses. Additionally, GC I/145, equipped with the troubled Caudron C.714, joined the front lines despite its known flaws. Grounded on 25 May by Aviation Minister Guy de Chambre due to engineering issues, the aircraft was pressed into service out of necessity. The rushed introduction of the Dewoitine D.520s left pilots without adequate training, though they welcomed the aircraft with enthusiasm. However, only 65 D.520s were operational on 5 June, limiting their impact.

As the campaign drew to a close, chaos consumed the French forces. The fall of Paris shattered morale, and Marshal Pétain's assumption of power marked the start of surrender negotiations. While this spared France complete German occupation, it created a significant fracture within the Allied effort.

Despite the collapse, French pilots achieved impressive individual success. At least 31 pilots scored six or more victories, with nine claiming ten or more. Most flew the American Curtiss H-75A. The top ace, Edmond Marin La Meslée, achieved 16 confirmed victories, leading a group of skilled but ultimately overwhelmed defenders.

Aircraft of GC I/2. Photo was taken in July 1940. In the foreground is MS.406 no. 946 flown by Polish pilot por. J. Brzeziński. (De Chasteigner coll. via B. Philippe.)

Bloch MB.151 no 370 of GC III/10 in flight. (SHAA)

Introduction

Jagdwaffe

The Germans allocated two *Luftflotten*, Nos. 2 and 3, to counter the Allied forces. Together, these formations fielded over 4,500 combat and transport aircraft – a staggering number for the time. This concentration of power enabled the Germans to quickly achieve the necessary air superiority. Their success rested largely on the principle of concentrating efforts in key areas and the exceptional combat skills of the *Jagdwaffe*, Göring's prized fighter force. At that time, German fighter aviation was arguably the best in the world, and Göring proudly showcased his "eagles" as the pinnacle of the *Luftwaffe's* capabilities.

As of 10 May 1940, the *Luftwaffe* officially included 13 fighter and 5 destroyer *Geschwadern*. This impressive force, by contemporary standards, should have consisted of nearly 2,000 aircraft. However, the reality was less dazzling. While there were 18 *Geschwadern* of single – and twin-engined fighters on paper, many of these units were still in the formative stages. Some existed only as placeholders, with little more than a name and minimal operational capability. Several *Geschwadern* comprised just a single *Gruppe* and lacked dedicated headquarters. Consequently, it would be inaccurate to regard them as fully functional formations.

Briefing before next mission, France 1940. One of the speakers is (probably) Oblt. G. Specht of I./ZG 26, with two kills as seen on the Bf 110 (U8+HH) in the foreground. (CAW)

Without the support of established units, smaller single – or two-*Gruppe* formations struggled to operate effectively. This led to the creation of ad hoc *Geschwadern*, hastily assembled for the campaign, whose cohesion and teamwork left much to be desired. A notable example is the unit centered on *Stab/JG 27*, which, as of 10 May, commanded *I/JG 21*, *I/JG 1*, *I/JG 51*, and *I/JG 27*. Meanwhile, *II/JG 27* reported to a different *Geschwader*, and *Stab/JG 51* managed *I/JG 26* and *I/JG 20*.

The Germans were acutely aware of this organizational chaos and the challenges it posed to deploying the *Jagdwaffe* as originally planned. As a result, following their victory in the French campaign, they initiated a large-scale reorganization of their fighter units during demobilization. Some *Geschwadern* designations disappeared from the order of battle, but the overall strength The summer of 1940 saw the disbandment of no fewer than six *Geschwadern*, with their components reorganized into additional *Gruppen* within existing units. This restructuring enabled *JG 27*, *JG 54*, and *JG 77* to reach full operational strength, while *JG 51* became the Luftwaffe's only four-*Gruppe Geschwader*.

Bf 109 E fighters of I/JG 3 at one of the German bases, spring 1940. Aircraft in typical camouflage of that period. (CAW)

By late April and early May, the vast majority of these units were concentrated along Germany's western border to face the Franco-British alliance, supported by "neutral" Belgium and the Netherlands. This concentration of fighter forces, along with other units, was made possible by several factors. In the spring of 1940, Germany faced no active enemies elsewhere, and the Eastern border remained secure with no imminent threats. Additionally, the French and British were conducting a passive campaign, making no effort to stretch German air defenses along the northern coast of the Third Reich. As a result, the Germans encountered no significant obstacles in massing their fighter units along the Rhine and Dutch border.

A total of 36 fighter and destroyer *Gruppen* were assembled in this area, comprising slightly over 1,600 aircraft. This force included nearly 1,250 *Bf 109Es* and over 300 *Bf 110s*. Additionally, there were over 30 reserve *Bf 109s* powered by *Jumo 210* engines and more than 35 obsolete *Ar 68s*. Despite organizational imperfections and technical challenges, this was an impressive force – not only in terms of numbers but also because the Allies lacked the capability to counter it with an equivalent number of equally capable aircraft.

The concentration of *Jagdwaffe* forces was further supported by a policy implemented by the high command in early 1940, which bolstered unit establishments with surplus aircraft. As a result, some *Gruppen*, nominally equipped with 40 aircraft, had as many as 45–47 machines. This ensured that even with ongoing engine issues, the number of serviceable Messerschmitts often reached 35. Consequently, many *Gruppen* were ready for maximum combat operations by 10 May.

However, there were notable exceptions to this readiness. In some batches of *Emils*, engineering problems severely impacted operational strength, leaving certain units able to field only half of their designated aircraft. For instance, *III/JG 26 "Schlageter"* had just 22 serviceable *Bf 109Es*, representing only 50% of its establishment. Despite these setbacks, the Germans deployed almost all available resources for the campaign against France. The only exceptions were *II/JG 77*, based in Norway, and *S* and *II/JG 3*, which remained in the Third Reich into mid-May.

The headquarters of *Luftflotte 2* oversaw 666 fighters and 145 destroyers. However, the serviceability rates were disappointing under the circumstances – short supply lines, ample preparation time, and units stationed at permanent bases. Only 72% of the fighters and 57% of the destroyers were operational. As a result, instead of deploying 842 aircraft, only 582 were serviceable, including 500 single-engined fighters. The true number, however, was even lower: 539 serviceable aircraft, of which 457 were *Bf 109Es*, as the *Jumo-powered Messerschmitts* and *Arados* were utterly obsolete by May 1940.

Similarly, the headquarters of *Luftflotte 3* managed 601 fighters and 174 destroyers. This formation faced comparable issues, with only 71% of its fighters and 73% of its destroyers operational. Consequently, of the 775 aircraft available, only 554 were serviceable, including 427 single-seat *Bf 109s*.

In total, the Germans fielded 1,298 fighters and 319 destroyers, of which 927 fighters and 209 destroyers were serviceable – a combined total of 1,136 operational aircraft. This was a for-

Bf 109 E-3, W.Nr 5102 of I./JG 77 Gruppen Adjutant. Aircraft with personal emblem and name "Kieki". See also colour profile on page 144. (Budesarchiv)

Bf 110C of Erg ZG over Paris. (Stratus coll.)

midable force compared to the French and British, but numbers alone did not tell the full story. What truly mattered was the quality of the *Jagdwaffe's* fighters.

The German fighter force was built around two aircraft types: the *Bf 109E* and the *Bf 110C*. From both tactical and engineering perspectives, these aircraft were near-perfect for their time, facing no equals over France until late May 1940, when RAF Spitfires entered the fray.

Between 10 May and 22 June, the Germans claimed to have shot down approximately 2,224[1] enemy aircraft in aerial combat, of which around 1,525 were credited to fighters. Additionally, German *Flak* units were credited with downing 854 enemy aircraft. On the other hand, the *Jagdwaffe* and *Zerstörerwaffe* suffered significant losses in France, with over 200 aircraft destroyed. Specifically, 169 *Bf 109s* and 90 *Bf 110s* were written off during May and June, totaling 259 aircraft.

Daily returns from the *Reichsluftfahrtministerium* (RLM) show that during operations from 10 May to 23 June, the Germans lost 244 *Bf 109s* and 110 *Bf 110s*, either seriously damaged or destroyed. While these losses were considerable, they were not enough to significantly weaken the Luftwaffe's overall combat effectiveness during the campaign.

Early production Hurricane (note two blade propeller), also abandoned on a French airfield. (T. J. Kopański coll.)

RAF

Before the declaration of war in September 1939, plans were made to deploy several RAF squadrons to France. Fighter Squadrons 1, 73, 85, and 87, equipped with Hurricanes, arrived in early September as part of the Air Component of British forces. While initially part of 60 Fighter Wing, 1 and 73 Squadrons were later assigned to the Advanced Air Striking Force (AASF) under 67 Fighter Wing. In November, Auxiliary Air Force Squadrons 607 and 615, flying Gladiators, joined under 61 Fighter Wing. These units transitioned to Hurricanes just before the German attack in May 1940 but lacked proficiency on the new aircraft.

The Hurricanes were not fully combat-ready, lacking essential features like pilot armor and self-sealing fuel tanks. Their tactics were outdated, focusing on bomber interceptions with rigid "vic" formations and poorly suited gun harmonization. However, *Sqn Ldr "Bull" Halahan* of 1 Squadron introduced a tighter convergence pattern at 250 yards, improving effectiveness.

By May 1940, the squadrons were based across France: 1 Sqn at Vassincourt, 73 Sqn at Rouvres, 85 Sqn at Lille/Seclin, and 87 Sqn with detachments at Senon. 607 and 615 Sqns were at Vitry-en-Artois, with 615 later moving to Abbeville for Hurricane re-equipping. During the "Phoney War," these units primarily intercepted reconnaissance aircraft and small bomber for-

The sparse remains of a Gladiator Mk I in France, destroyed on the ground, is inspected by a German soldier after the British had left. (T. J. Kopański coll.)

1 By 4 June, German claims totaled 1,841 aerial victories, with 1,142 attributed to the Jagdwaffe. After 3 June, an additional 383 victories were reported, although the specific units or pilots responsible were not detailed. The OKW (*Oberkommando der Wehrmacht*) attributed these 383 victories entirely to the fighters, bringing the total fighter claims to 1,525. However, discrepancies exist between the OKW figures and actual data, for reasons that remain unclear. For instance, victory claims on 10 May were reportedly reduced by half, while those for 14 May were overclaimed by approximately 100%. Such inconsistencies highlight the challenges in verifying wartime aerial victory claims, especially when relying on incomplete or exaggerated reports.

mations, with 1 and 73 Squadrons claiming the majority of victories, including 1 Sqn's first on 30 October 1939 and *Flg Off E.J. "Cobber" Kain* of 73 Sqn becoming the RAF's first ace.

By 10 May, RAF fighters claimed 60 confirmed victories, 16 probables, and 22 damaged, though Luftwaffe records suggest only 35 losses. Recognition issues plagued all forces, with some RAF aircraft being mistaken for the enemy by both French and British ground and air units. AASF Hurricanes adopted French rudder stripes and single aircraft letters to address this.

The German attack on 10 May brought reinforcements from UK-based squadrons, including 3, 79, 501, and later 504 Sqns, as well as elements from 11 Group. Of the 452 Hurricanes deployed, only 66 returned to the UK, with most ground equipment lost. RAF fighter squadrons claimed 500 victories and over 120 probables in May, against 215 Hurricanes shot down. Actual Luftwaffe losses to French-based RAF units totaled 299 aircraft destroyed and 65+ heavily damaged. Casualties included 56 pilots killed, 36 wounded, and 18 taken prisoner.

Italian-French Air Operations

The *1ª Squadra Aerea* was responsible for supporting the two Italian armies. It included four fighter regiments, two of which – the *3° Stormo* and *53° Stormo* – were equipped with Fiat CR.42 *Falco* biplanes. The *3° Stormo's 18° Gruppo* operated from Novi Ligule and Albenga airfields, while *23° Gruppo* was based at Cervere. The *53° Stormo's* units, *150° Gruppo* and *151° Gruppo*, were stationed at Caselle Torinese and Casablanca airfields, respectively. Additionally, the *9° Gruppo*, also flying CR.42s, was based at Gorizia.

The *54° Stormo* operated the more advanced Macchi MC.200 *Saetta* monoplane fighters. Its two *gruppi – 152°* and *153°* – were stationed at Airasca and Vergiate airfields, respectively. Each *gruppo* comprised three *squadriglie* and was tasked with escorting twin-engine Fiat BR.20 *Cicogna* bombers.

For operations against France, elements of the *3ª Squadra Aerea* were deployed as follows:

The *1° Stormo*, consisting of *17° Gruppo* and *157° Gruppo*, both equipped with CR.42 and CR.32 *Chirri* biplanes, operated from Palermo and Trapani airfields.

The *6° Gruppo Autonomo*, based in Catania, operated MC.200 aircraft.

Other units from the *3ª Squadra Aerea* also participated, including the *51° Stormo*, equipped with Fiat G.50 *Freccia* monoplane fighters. Its two *gruppi – 20°* and *21°* – operated from Ciampino, while *22° Gruppo* of the *52° Stormo*, based at Capodichino, flew G.50 and CR.32 aircraft. These units carried out attacks on Corsica, patrolled French territorial waters, and escorted bombing raids on Tunisia.

The *6° Stormo* was later divided, with its CR.32 aircraft redeployed to airfields in Sardinia, at Monserrato and Alghero.

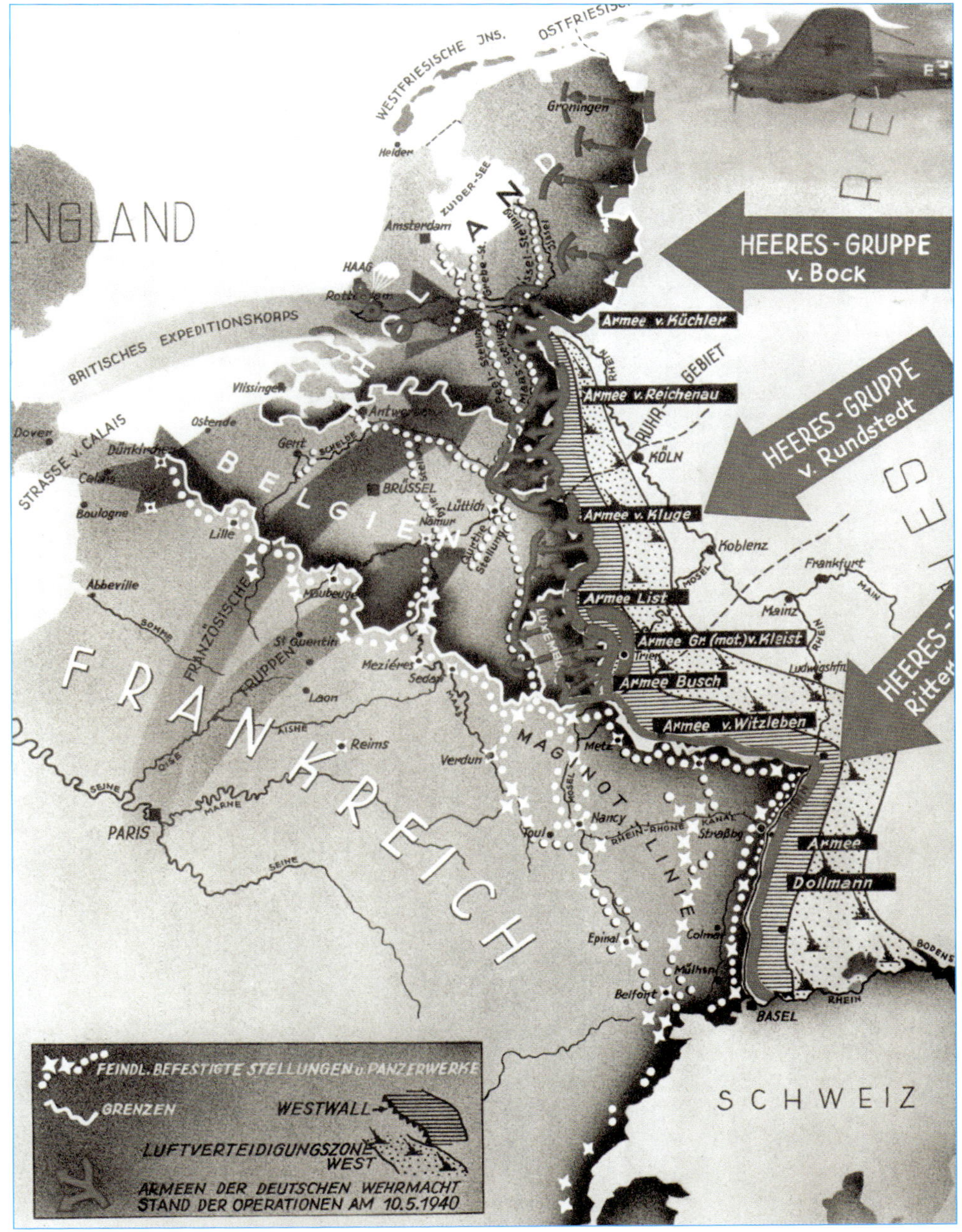

Map of German attack on Low Countries. Map was originally published in "Wehrmachtberichte Weltgeschichte, Der Krieg 1939/40" by Verlag Die Wehrmacht K. G., Berlin, 1941.

Morane-Saulnier MS.405 no. 8 (N-258), CIC Chartres. Emblem and codes of the 2nd escadrille of the GC I/7 (previous operator). Chartres June 1940.

- *Vert kaki foncé* uppersurface, *gris bleu clair marine* undersurface.

Morane-Saulnier MS.406 No. 46 (N357) Escadre de Marche d'Afrique du Nord (North African Marching Squadron), Oran 1939.

- *Vert foncé*, *Brun foncé*, *Gris-bleu foncé* – uppersurfaces with *Gris-bleu clair* undersurfaces.

Morane-Saulnier MS.405 no. 8 (N-258), CIC Chartres. Chartres June 1940.

Morane-Saulnier MS.406 no. 882 (L-911) code I, CIC Montpellier.

- *Vert foncé*, *Brun foncé*, *Gris-bleu foncé* – uppersurfaces with *Gris-bleu clair* undersurfaces.

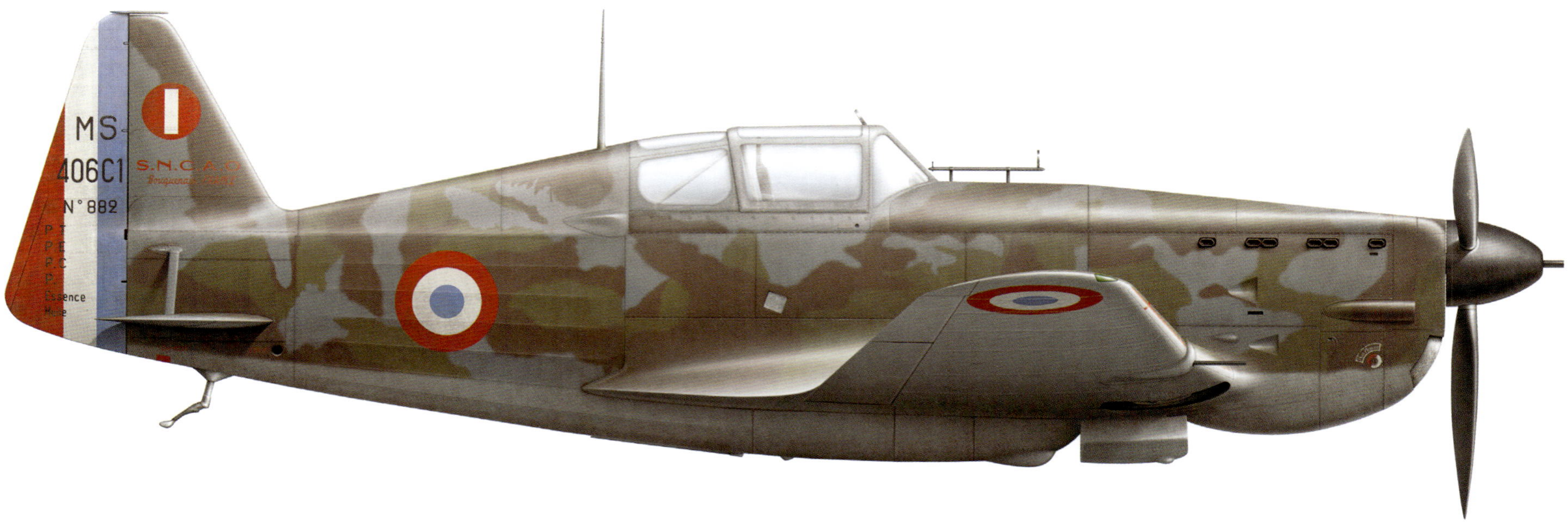

Karolina Hołda/Artur Juszczak

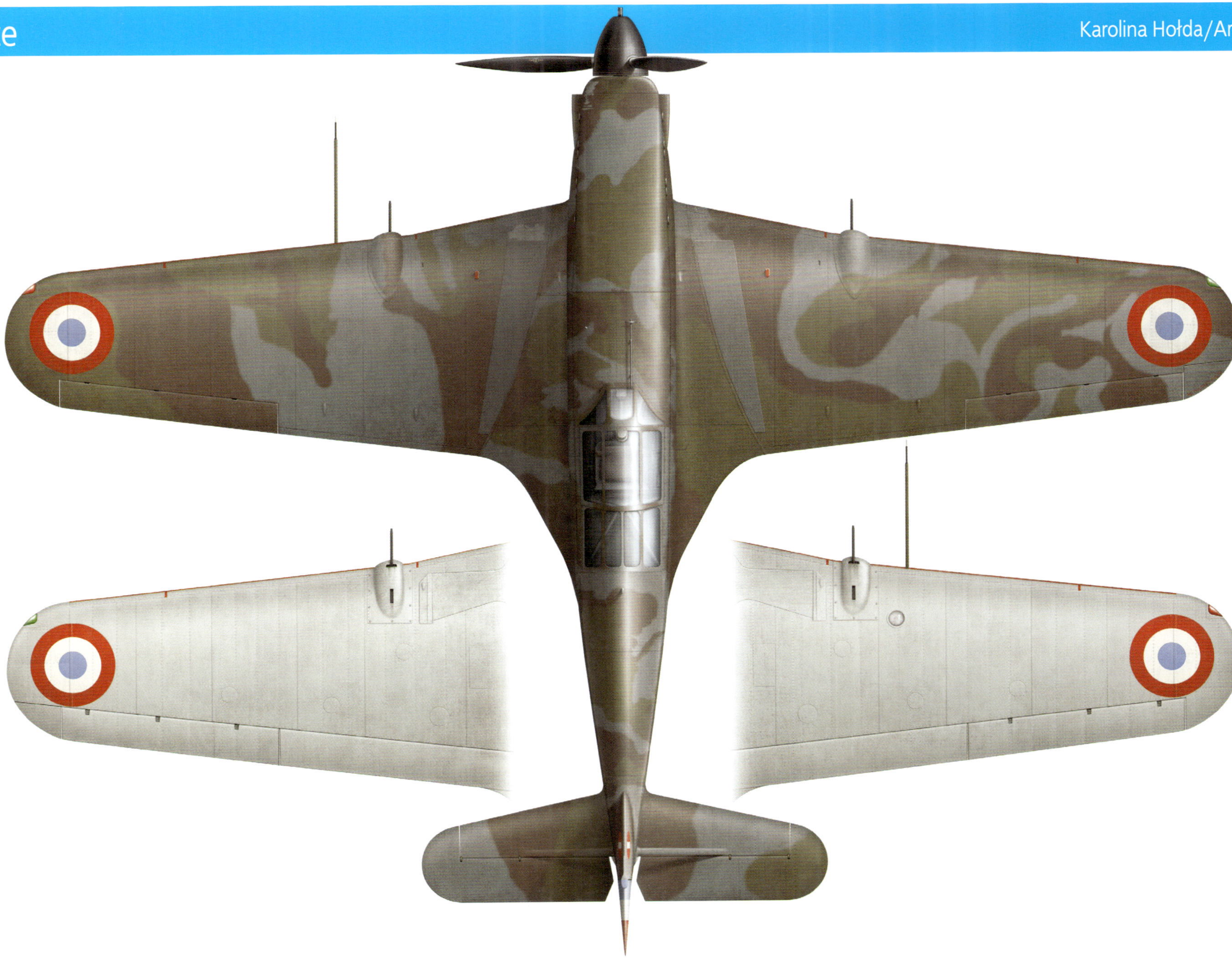

Morane-Saulnier MS.406 No. 546 (N964) of GC III/3 5th escadrille, pilot Sergent Josef Hubacek, aircraft damaged in combat 11 May 1940.

- *Vert foncé, Brun foncé, Gris-bleu foncé* – uppersurfaces with *Gris-bleu clair* undersurfaces.

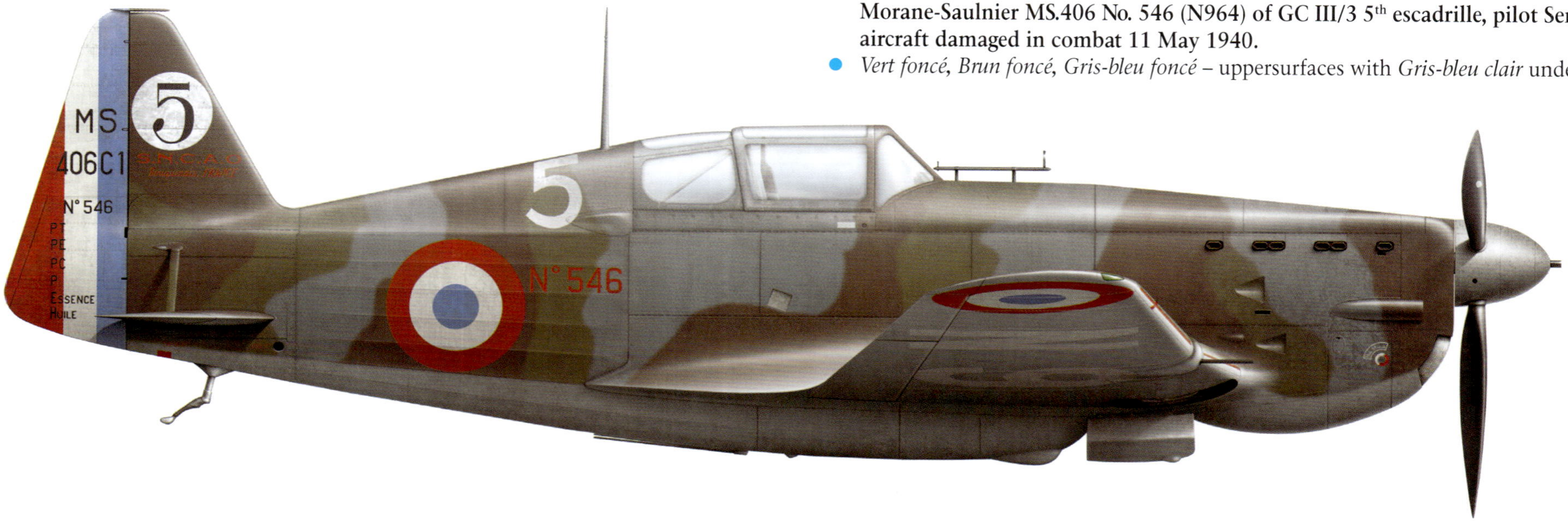

Morane-Saulnier MS.406 No. 795 (L824) of GC III/6 6th escadrille, pilot Adjutant Jean Bertrand, Vitry-le-François airfield, December 1939/January 1940.

- *Vert foncé, Brun foncé, Gris-bleu foncé, Tierra Sienne* – uppersurfaces with *Gris-bleu clair* undersurfaces.

Morane-Saulnier MS.406 No. 1053 (L643) of GC I/6 1st escadrille, pilot Capitaine Mauvier, Marignane airfield, January 1940.

- *Vert foncé, Brun foncé, Gris-bleu foncé* – uppersurfaces with *Gris-bleu clair* undersurfaces.

Morane-Saulnier MS.406 No. 966 of GC I/2 1st escadrille, Damaged 5 June 1940. Damblain airfield, May 1940.

- *Vert foncé, Brun foncé, Gris-bleu foncé* – uppersurfaces with *Gris-bleu clair* undersurfaces.

Karolina Hołda/Artur Juszczak

Morane-Saulnier MS.406 no. 1031 (L-621) code I, Montpellier Groupof of the GC III/1, 5th escadrille. Pilot Lt Kazimierz Bursztyn.

- *Vert foncé*, *Brun foncé*, *Gris-bleu foncé* – uppersurfaces with *Gris-bleu clair* undersurfaces.

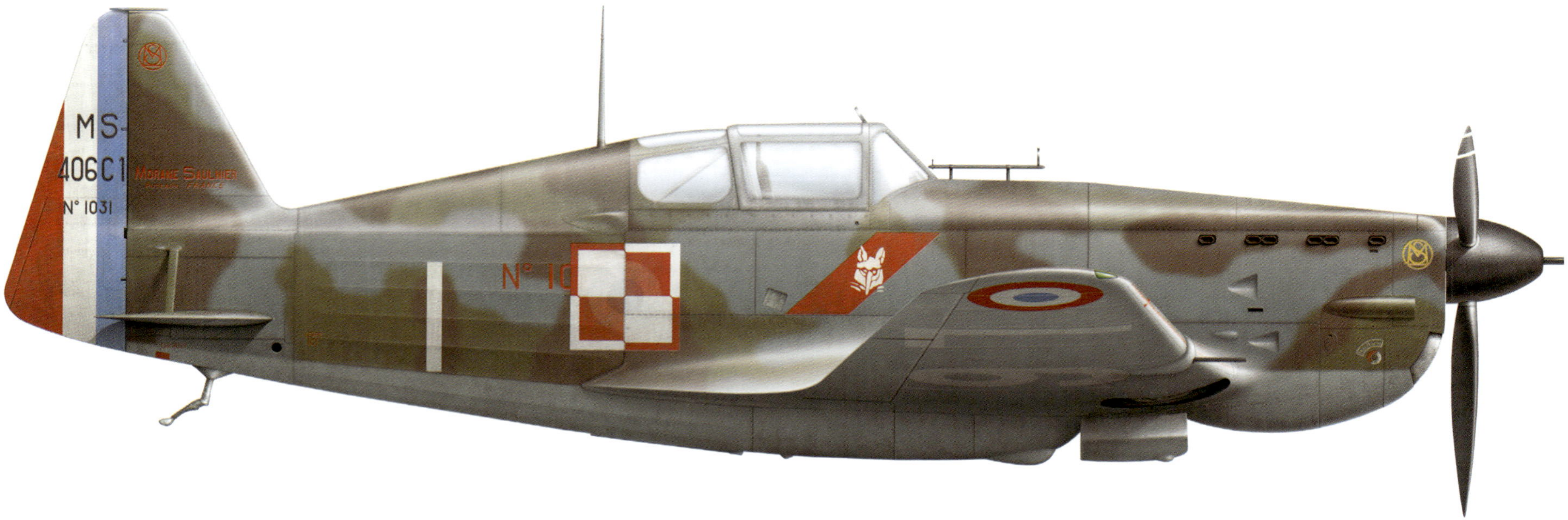

Morane-Saulnier MS.406 no. 1031 (L-621) code I, Montpellier Groupof of the GC III/1, 5th escadrille. Pilot Lt Kazimierz Bursztyn.

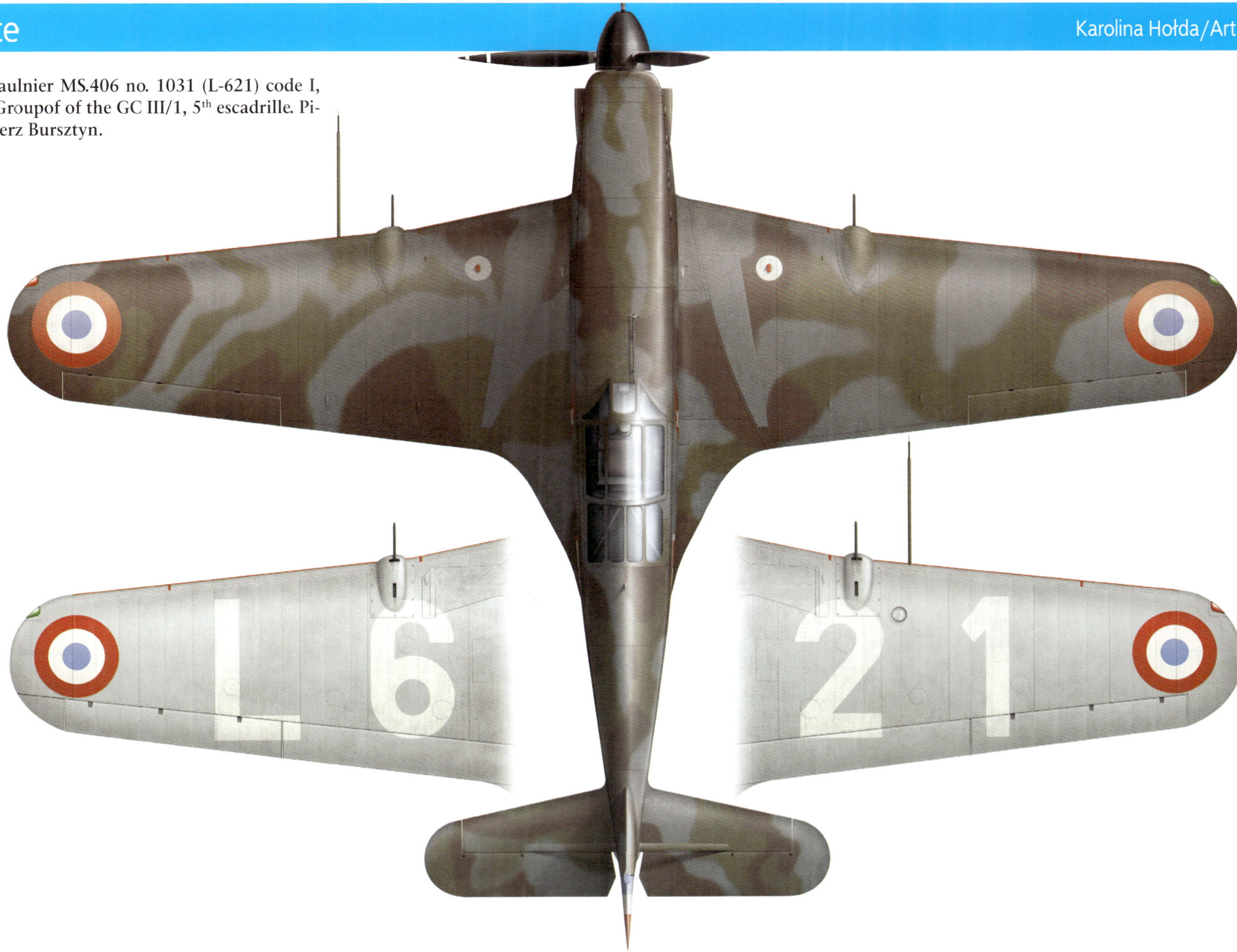

Dewoitine D.520 No. 49 of GC I/6, pilot état-major Capitaine Rivalls-Maezères, Lognes airfield, 8 June 1940

- *Vert foncé, Brun foncé, Gris-bleu foncé* – uppersurfaces with *Gris-bleu clair* undersurfaces.

Dewoitine D.520 No. 98 of GC I/3 1st escadlille, pilot Sergent-chef Paul Bellefin, Wez airfield, 15 May 1940

- *Vert foncé, Brun foncé, Gris-bleu foncé* – uppersurfaces with *Gris-bleu clair* undersurfaces.

Dewoitine D.520 No. 115 of GC I/3 2nd escadlille, pilot Sous-lieutenant Boutarel, the plane crashed on May 1940 in Beugneux.

- *Vert foncé*, *Brun foncé*, *Gris-bleu foncé* – uppersurfaces with *Gris-bleu clair* undersurfaces.

Dewoitine D.520 No. 242 of GC I/7 3rd escadlille, pilot Cdr Mieczysław Mümler, Ounans airfield, 15 June 1940

- *Vert foncé*, *Brun foncé*, *Gris-bleu foncé* – uppersurfaces with *Gris-bleu clair* undersurfaces.

Dewoitine D.520 No. 242 of GC II/7 3rd escadlille, pilot S/Lt Georges Valentin, Ounans airfield, 15 June 1940

- *Vert foncé*, *Brun foncé*, *Gris-bleu foncé* – uppersurfaces with *Gris-bleu clair* undersurfaces.

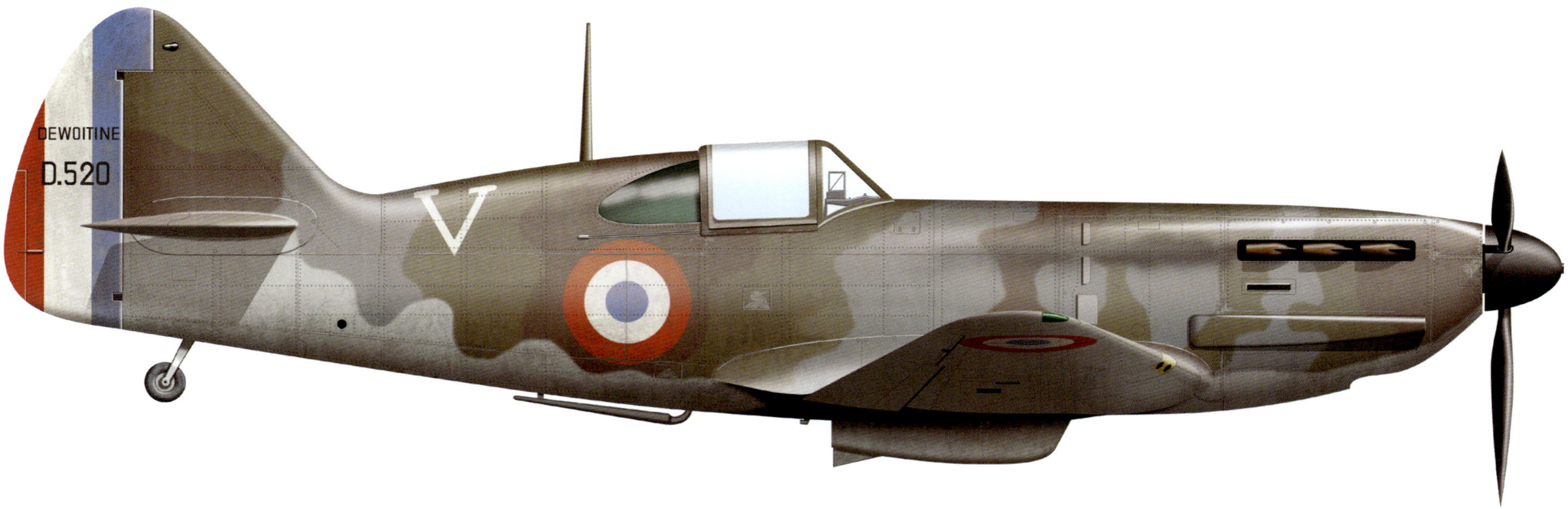

Dewoitine D.520 No. 242 of GC II/7 3rd escadlille, pilot S/Lt Georges Valentin, Ounans airfield, 15 June 1940

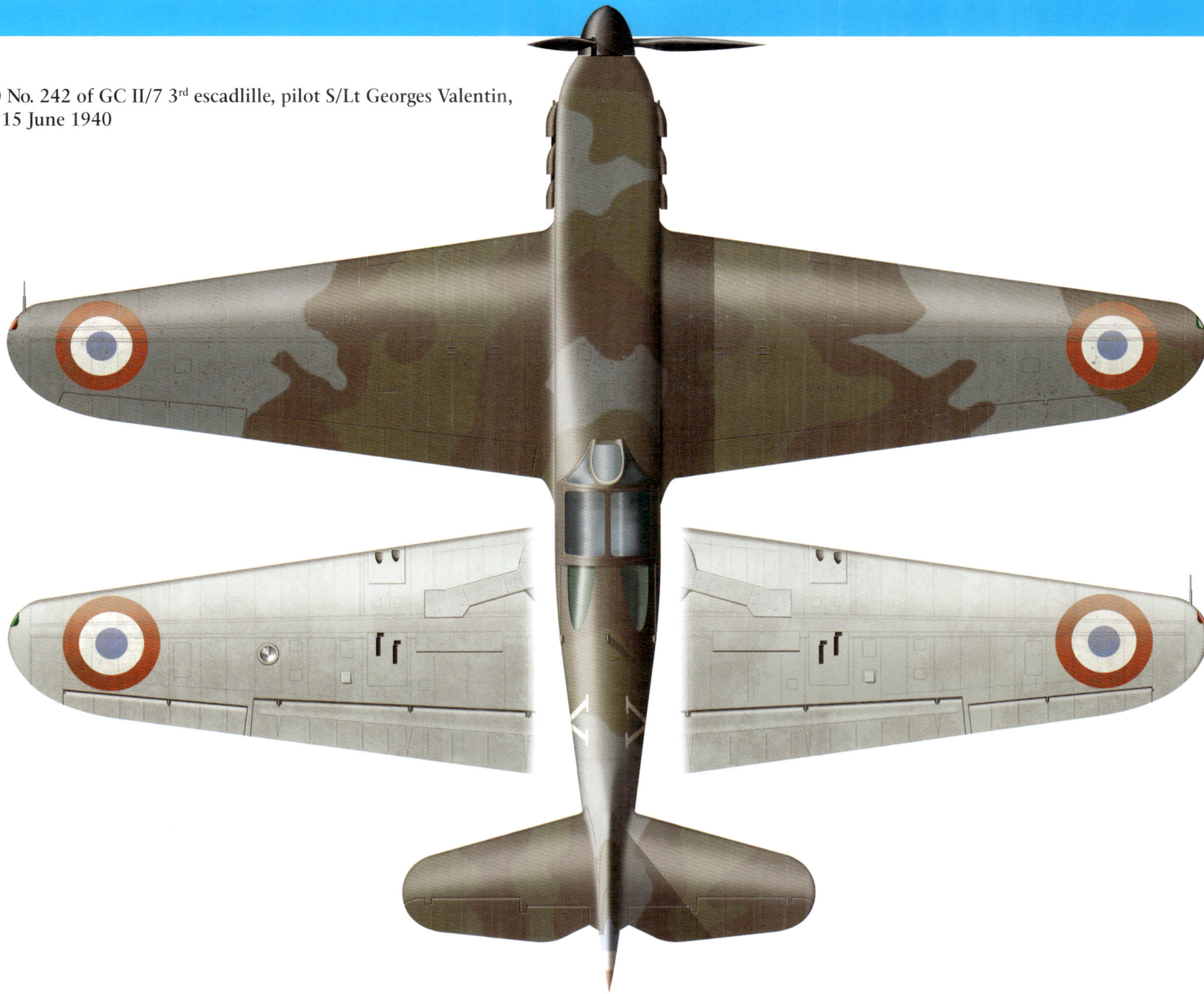

Dewoitine D.520 No. 266 of II/7 4th escadrille, pilot S/Lt. Renè Pomier-Layrargues, May 1940.

- *Vert foncé, Brun foncé, Gris-bleu foncé* – uppersurfaces with *Gris-bleu clair* undersurfaces.

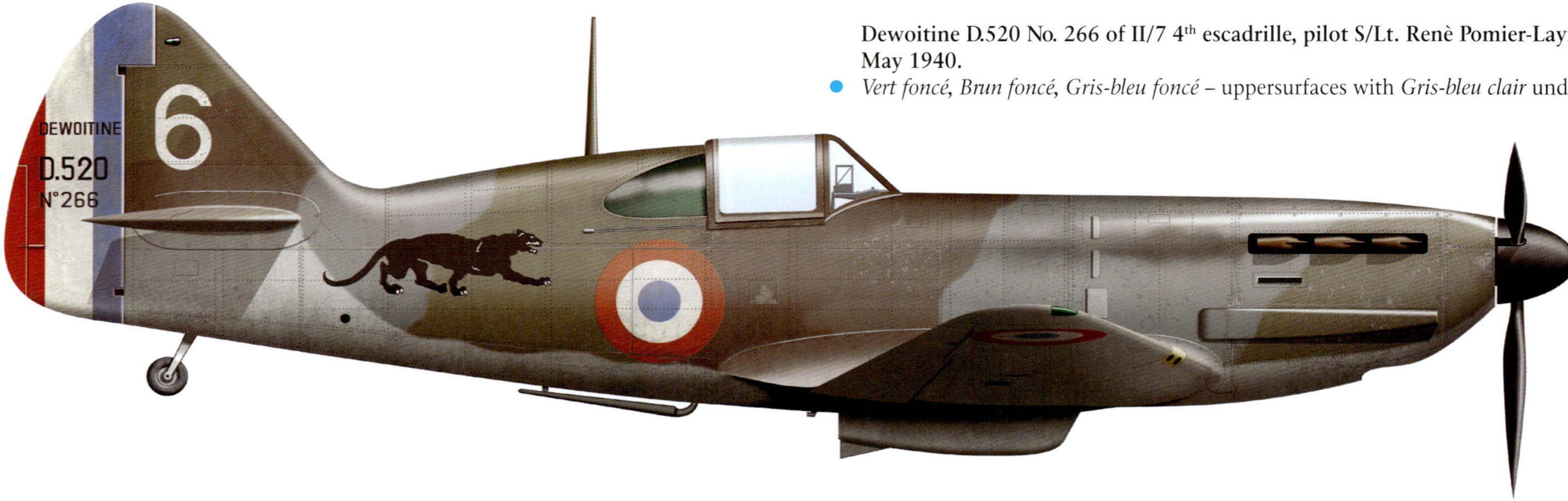

Dewoitine D.520 No. 273 of II/7 4th escadrille, pilot Adjutant-Chef Denis Ponteins Meaux-Esbly airfield, 5 June 1940.

- *Vert foncé, Brun foncé, Gris-bleu foncé* – uppersurfaces with *Gris-bleu clair* undersurfaces.

Dewoitine D.520 No. 273 of II/3 2nd escadrille, pilot A/C Bouton, June 1940.

- *Vert foncé, Brun foncé, Gris-bleu foncé* – uppersurfaces with *Gris-bleu clair* undersurfaces.

Dewoitine D.520 No. ? Escadrille AC1, Campo dell'Oro, June 1940.

- *Vert foncé, Brun foncé, Gris-bleu foncé* – uppersurfaces with *Gris-bleu clair* undersurfaces.

Curtiss H-75A1 n°26 (X825), GC I/5, 2nd escadrille, May 1940.

- *Vert foncé*, *Brun foncé*, *Gris-bleu foncé* – uppersurfaces with *Gris-bleu clair* undersurfaces.

Curtiss H-75A1 n°26 (X825), GC I/5, 2nd escadrille, May 1940.

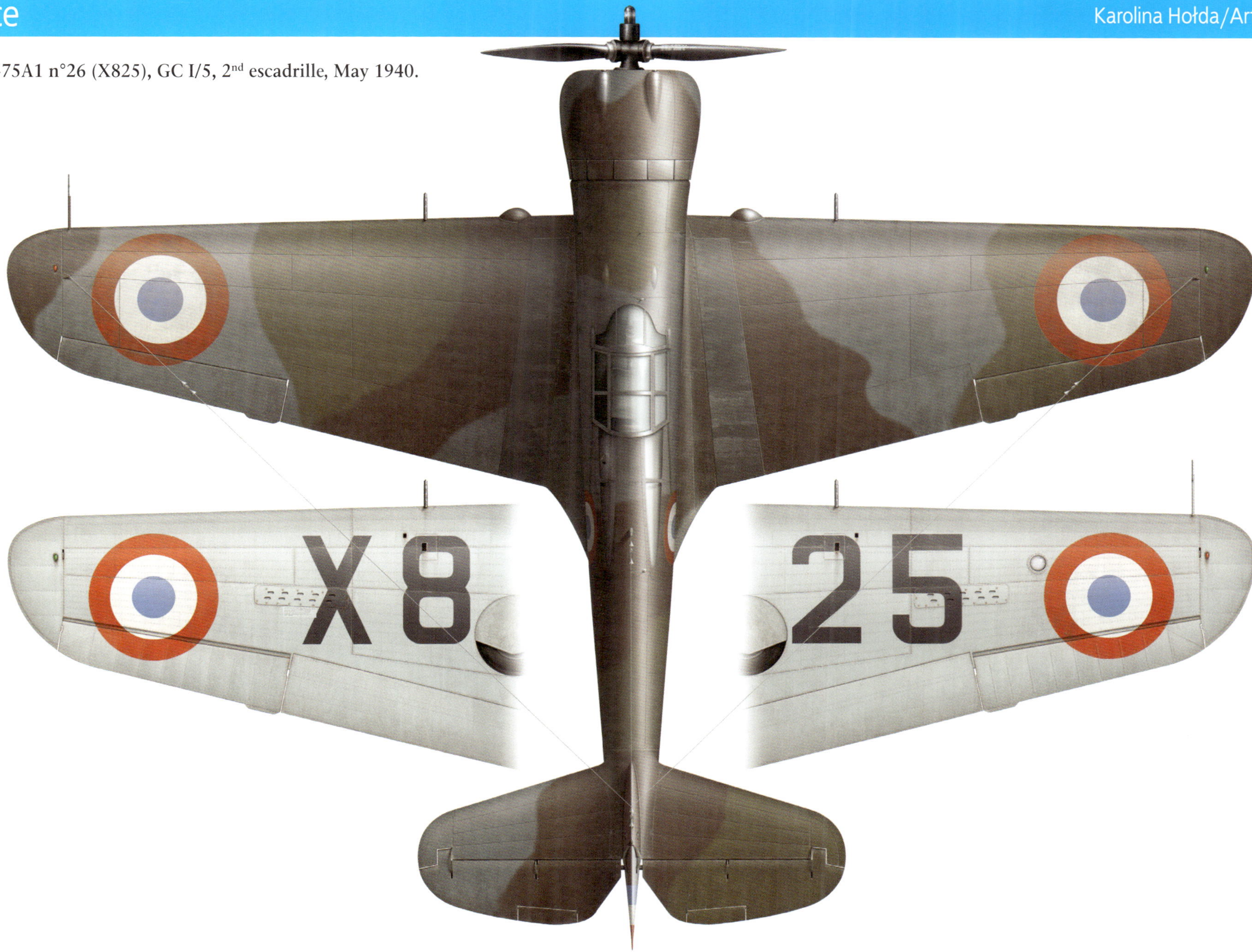

Curtiss H-75A.1 no. 12 (X811), DAT Bourges, May–June 1940.

- *Vert foncé, Brun foncé, Gris-bleu foncé* – uppersurfaces with *Gris-bleu clair* undersurfaces.

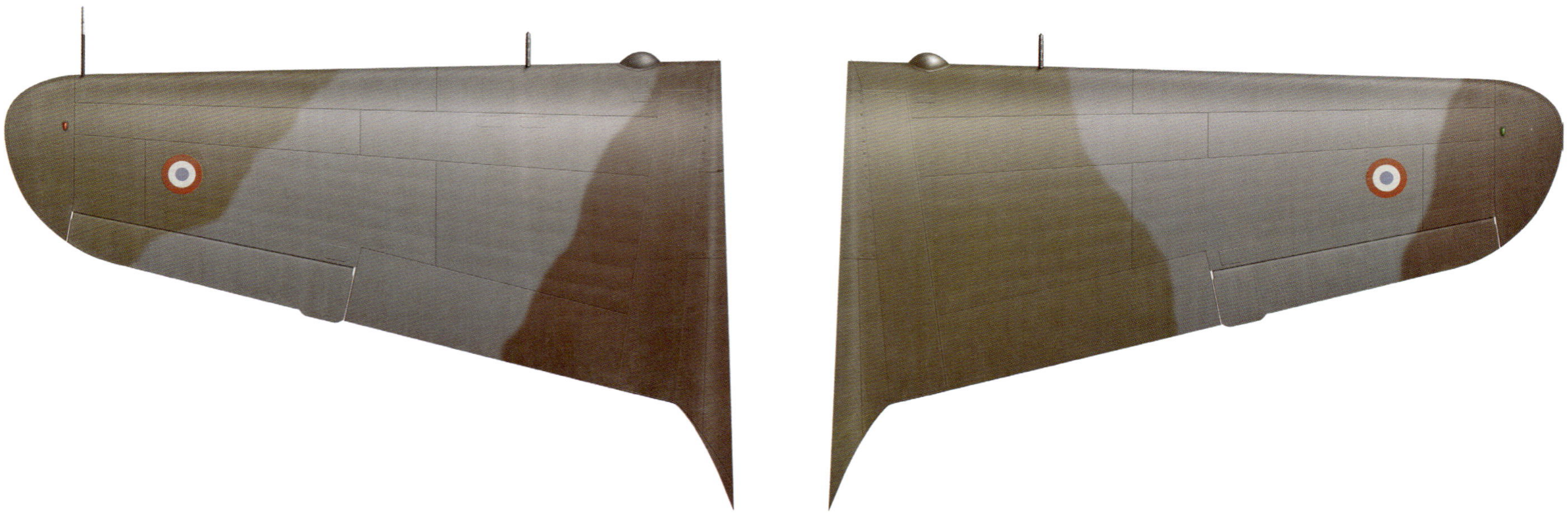

Curtiss H-75A1 n°91 (X890), GC II/4, 3rd escadrille, May 1940.

- *Vert foncé, Brun foncé, Gris-bleu foncé* – uppersurfaces with *Gris-bleu clair* undersurfaces.

Curtiss H-75A1 n°99, GC I/4, 2nd escadrille, 1 May 1940.

- *Vert foncé, Brun foncé, Gris-bleu foncé* – uppersurfaces with *Gris-bleu clair* undersurfaces.

Curtiss H-75A2 n°125 (U025), GC I/5, 1st escadrille, June 1940.

- *Vert foncé, Brun foncé, Gris-bleu foncé* – uppersurfaces with *Gris-bleu clair* undersurfaces.

Curtiss H-75A2 n°125 (U025), GC I/5, 1st escadrille, June 1940.

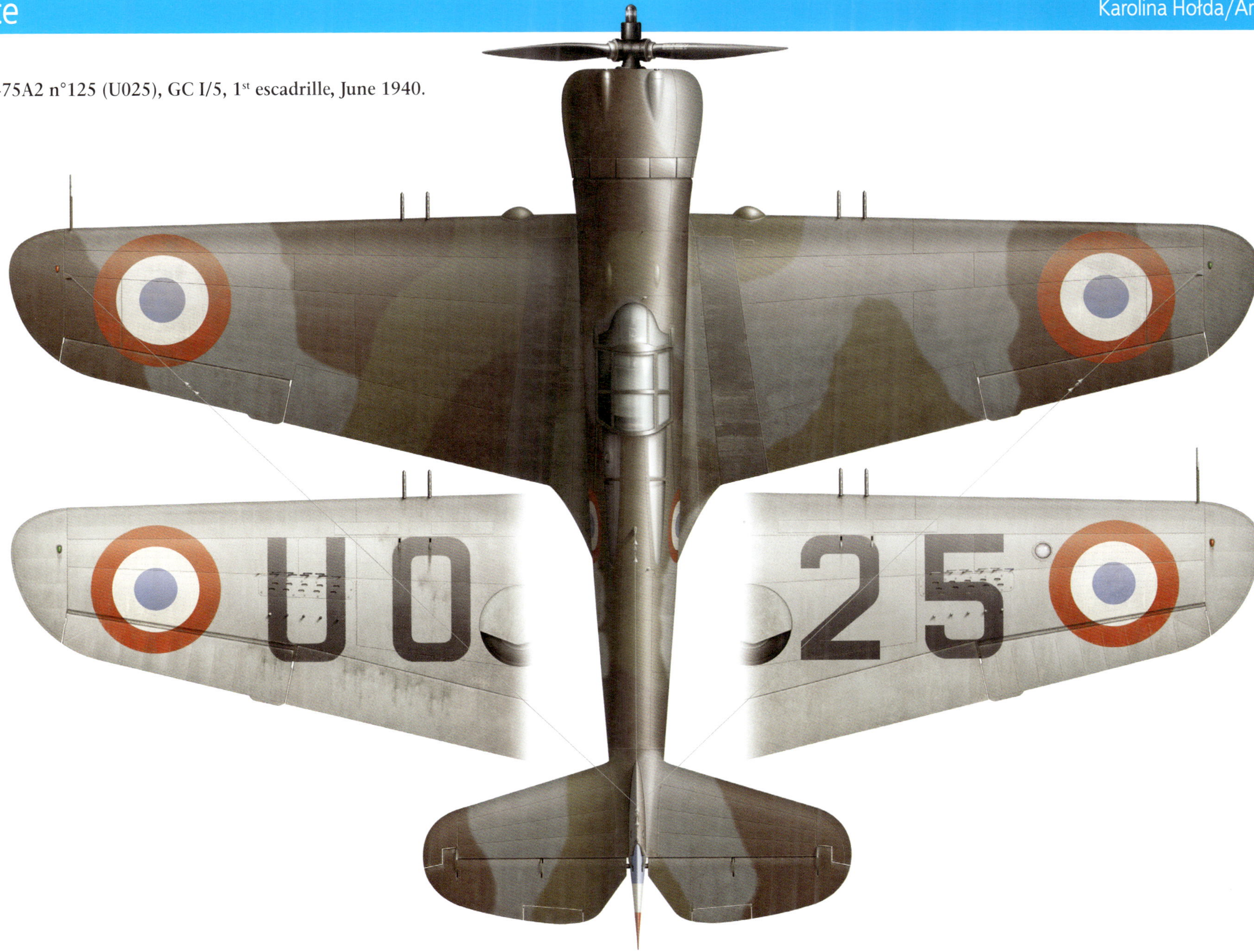

Curtiss H-75A2 n°107 (U007), GCD I/55, June 1940.
Personal aircraft of Jan Zumbach.

- *Vert foncé*, *Brun foncé*, *Gris-bleu foncé* – uppersurfaces with *Gris-bleu clair* undersurfaces.

Curtiss H-75A2 n°140 (U040), CIC of Chartres, april 1940.

- *Vert foncé*, *Brun foncé*, *Gris-bleu foncé* – uppersurfaces with *Gris-bleu clair* undersurfaces.

Curtiss H-75A2 no. 183 (U083), pilot Lt Col. Marcel Haegelen, DAT Bourges, May–June 1940.

- *Vert foncé, Brun foncé, Gris-bleu foncé* – uppersurfaces with *Gris-bleu clair* undersurfaces.

Possible alternative appearance of the fin with a full-colour Polish marking.

Curtiss H-75A3 n°217, GC I/5, 1st escadrille, June 1940.

- *Vert foncé, Brun foncé, Gris-bleu foncé* – uppersurfaces with *Gris-bleu clair* undersurfaces.

Caudron-Renault CR.714 no. 8584 (I-242) of GC 1/145 2nd esscadrille, pilot 2nd Lt Czesław Główczyński. Rochefort, June 1940.

- *Vert foncé, Brun foncé, Gris-bleu foncé* – uppersurfaces with *Gris-bleu clair* undersurfaces.

Caudron-Renault CR.714 no. 8584 (I-242) of GC 1/145 2nd esscadrille, pilot 2nd Lt Czesław Główczyński. Rochefort, June 1940.

Caudron-Renault CR.714 no. 8543, code no. 10 (I-201)of GC 1/145 2nd escadrille, pilot LAC Andrzej Niewiara. Dreux, June 1940.

- *Vert foncé*, *Brun foncé*, *Gris-bleu foncé* – uppersurfaces with *Gris-bleu clair* undersurfaces.

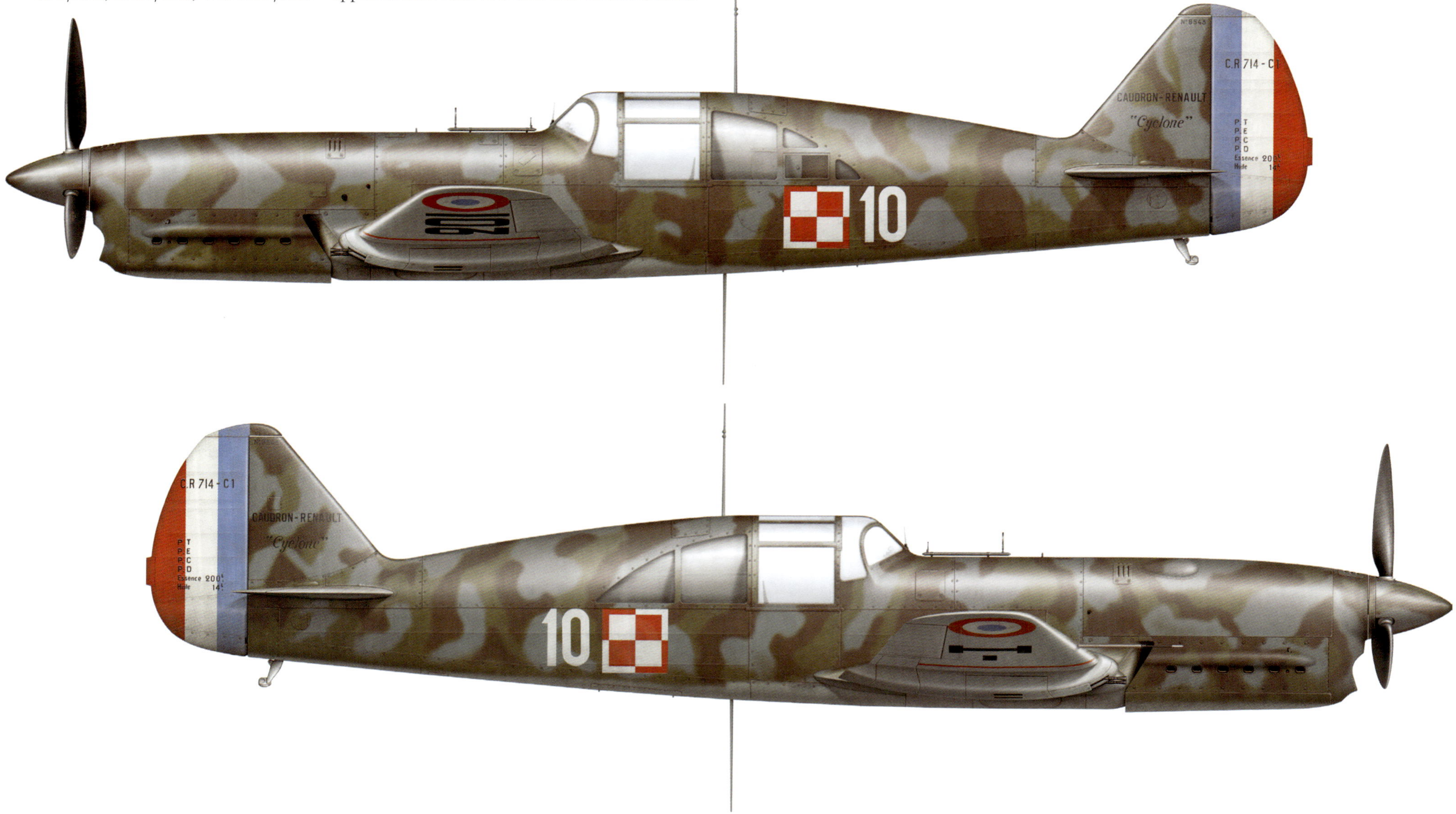

Caudron-Renault CR.714 no. 8543, code no. 10 (I-201)of GC 1/145 2nd escadrille, pilot LAC Andrzej Niewiara. Dreux, June 1940.

Bloch MB.152, no. 105 (Y-592), code no. 4 of the GC II/8, pilot por. Ludwik Paszkiewicz, Villacoublay, 24 May 1940.

- *Vert foncé, Brun foncé, Gris-bleu foncé* – uppersurfaces with *Gris-bleu clair* undersurfaces.

Bloch MB.152, no. 149 (Y-636), code no. 28 of GC 1/145 (ex-GC I/8 aircraft), June 1940.

- *Vert foncé, Brun foncé, Gris-bleu foncé – uppersurfaces with Gris-bleu clair undersurfaces.*

Bloch MB.152, no. 197 (Y-684), code no. 4 of GC III/10, pilot plut. Marian Rytka, Les Grandes Chapelles, 10 June 1940.

- *Vert foncé, Brun foncé, Gris-bleu foncé* – uppersurfaces with *Gris-bleu clair* undersurfaces.

Bloch MB.152, no. 202 (Y-689) of GC 1/145 (ex-GC I/8), pilot ppor. Marian Łukaszewicz, June 1940.

- *Vert foncé, Brun foncé, Gris-bleu foncé* – uppersurfaces with *Gris-bleu clair* undersurfaces.

Bloch MB.152, no. 622, code no. 15, 'IRAŚ' of GC II/6 3rd escadrille, pilot plut. Eugeniusz Szaposznikow, Châteauroux-Deols, May 1940.

- *Vert foncé, Brun foncé, Gris-bleu foncé* – uppersurfaces with *Gris-bleu clair* undersurfaces.

Bloch MB.152, no. 656, code no. 1 of DAT Châteauroux, pilot por. Zdzisław Henneberg, June 1940.

- *Vert foncé, Brun foncé, Gris-bleu foncé* – uppersurfaces with *Gris-bleu clair* undersurfaces.

MB.152 no. 656 with the white code number 1 on the fuselage. The number, probably applied during late May/early June, survived after the aircraft arrived in England (as opposed to the other number applied on the fin), when the French markings were replaced with RAF insignia.

- *Vert foncé, Brun foncé, Gris-bleu foncé* – uppersurfaces with *Gris-bleu clair* undersurfaces.

Bloch MB.152, no. 658, code no. 3 of the DAT Châteauroux, pilot kpr. Ryszard Lewczyński, June 1940.

- *Vert foncé, Brun foncé, Gris-bleu foncé* – uppersurfaces with *Gris-bleu clair* undersurfaces.

Koolhoven FK.58 no. 11 of Eskadra Myśliwska of kpt. Walerian Jasionowski. June 1940.

- *Vert foncé (Kaki), Terre foncée, Gris bleu foncé* – uppersurfaces with *gris bleu clair* undersurface.

Koolhoven FK.58 no. 17 of Eskadra Myśliwska of kpt. Walerian Jasionowski. June 1940.

- *Vert foncé (Kaki), Terre foncée, Gris bleu foncé* – uppersurfaces with *gris bleu clair* undersurface.

Potez 631 c/n 21 (X-720), Escadrille AC1, Aéronautique Navale, Hyères- le Palyvestre, June 1940.

- *Vert foncé (Kaki), Terre foncée, Gris bleu foncé* – uppersurfaces with *gris bleu clair* undersurface.

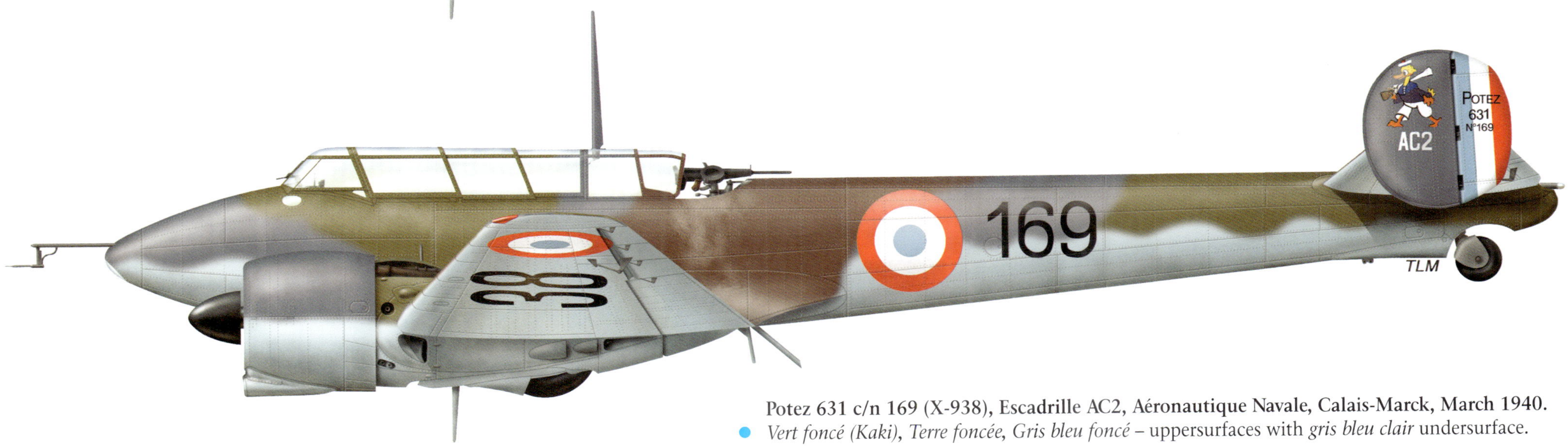

Potez 631 c/n 169 (X-938), Escadrille AC2, Aéronautique Navale, Calais-Marck, March 1940.

- *Vert foncé (Kaki), Terre foncée, Gris bleu foncé* – uppersurfaces with *gris bleu clair* undersurface.

Potez 631 c/n 73 (X-644), ECN 1/13, Meaux-Villenoy, spring 1940.

- *Vert foncé (Kaki), Terre foncée, Gris bleu foncé* – uppersurfaces with *gris bleu clair* undersurface.

Potez 631 c/n 73 (X-644), ECN 1/13, Meaux-Villenoy, spring 1940.

Potez 631 c/n 47 (X-618), Escadrille AC1, Aéronautique Navale, Cherbourg, June 1940.

- *Vert foncé (Kaki), Terre foncée, Gris bleu foncé* – uppersurfaces with *gris bleu clair* undersurface.

Potez 631 c/n 58 (X-629), Istres, April 1940.

- *Vert foncé (Kaki), Terre foncée, Gris bleu foncé* – uppersurfaces with *gris bleu clair* undersurface.

Karolina Hołda/Artur Juszczak

Hawker Hurricane Mk. I, code P, PADDY III of No. 73 Squadron RAF, pilot PO Edgar James Kain, France April 1940.

- Dark Green, Dark Earth– uppersurfaces with Day Night undersurface.

Hawker Hurricane Mk. I, serial P2569, code D of No. 73 Squadron RAF, France April 1940.

- Dark Green, Dark Earth– uppersurfaces with Day Night undersurface.

Hawker Hurricane Mk. I, serial P2575, code J of No. 73 Squadron RAF, France April 1940.

- Dark Green, Dark Earth– uppersurfaces with Day Night undersurface.

Hawker Hurricane Mk. I, serial L2047, LK-H of No. 87 Squadron RAF, Lille-Seclin, France May 1940.

- Dark Green, Dark Earth– uppersurfaces with Day Night undersurface.

Hawker Hurricane Mk. I, serial L2047, LK-H of No. 87 Squadron RAF, Lille-Seclin, France May 1940.

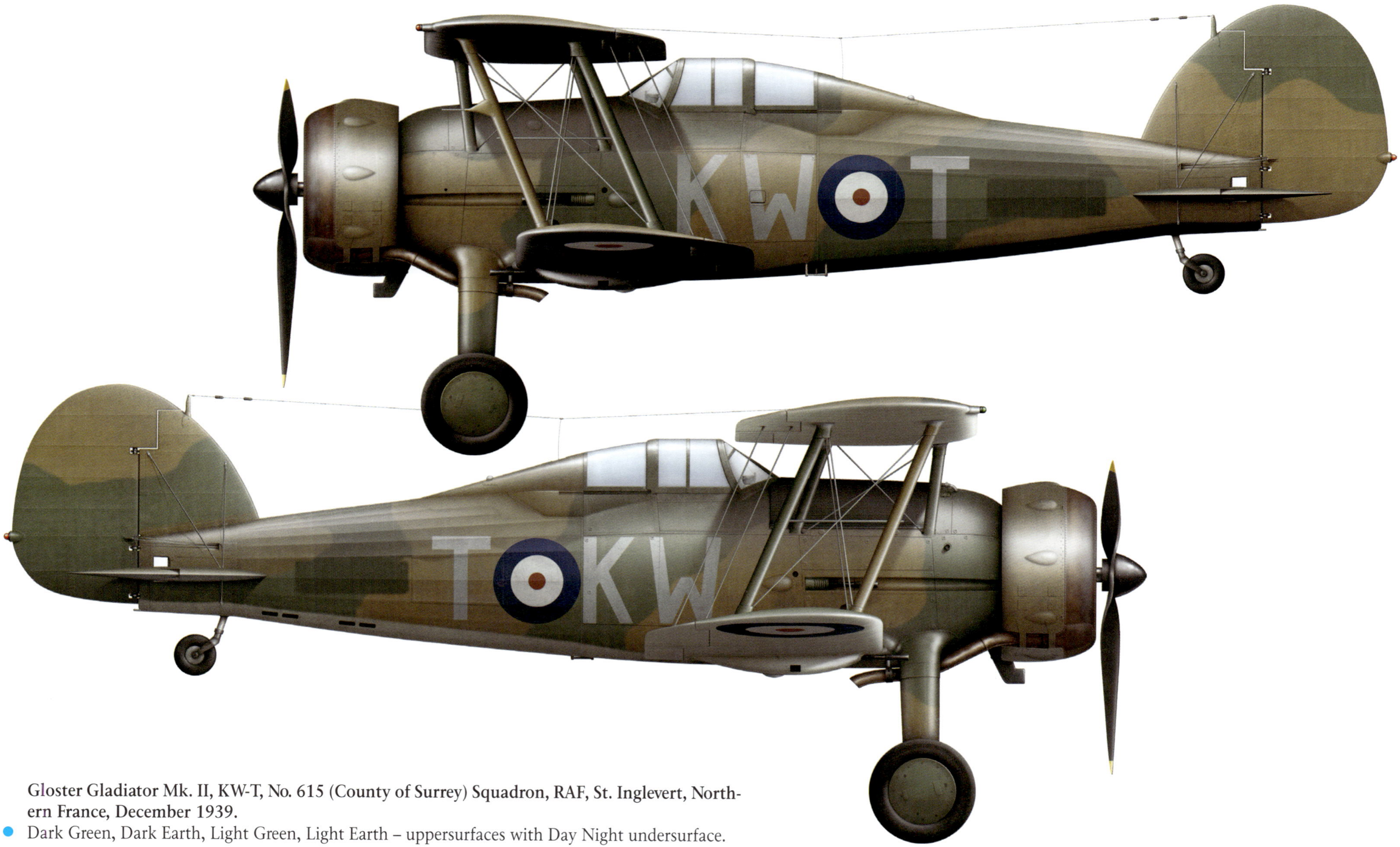

Gloster Gladiator Mk. II, KW-T, No. 615 (County of Surrey) Squadron, RAF, St. Inglevert, Northern France, December 1939.

- Dark Green, Dark Earth, Light Green, Light Earth – uppersurfaces with Day Night undersurface.

Gloster Gladiator Mk. II, KW-T, No. 615 (County of Surrey) Squadron, RAF, St. Inglevert, Northern France, December 1939.

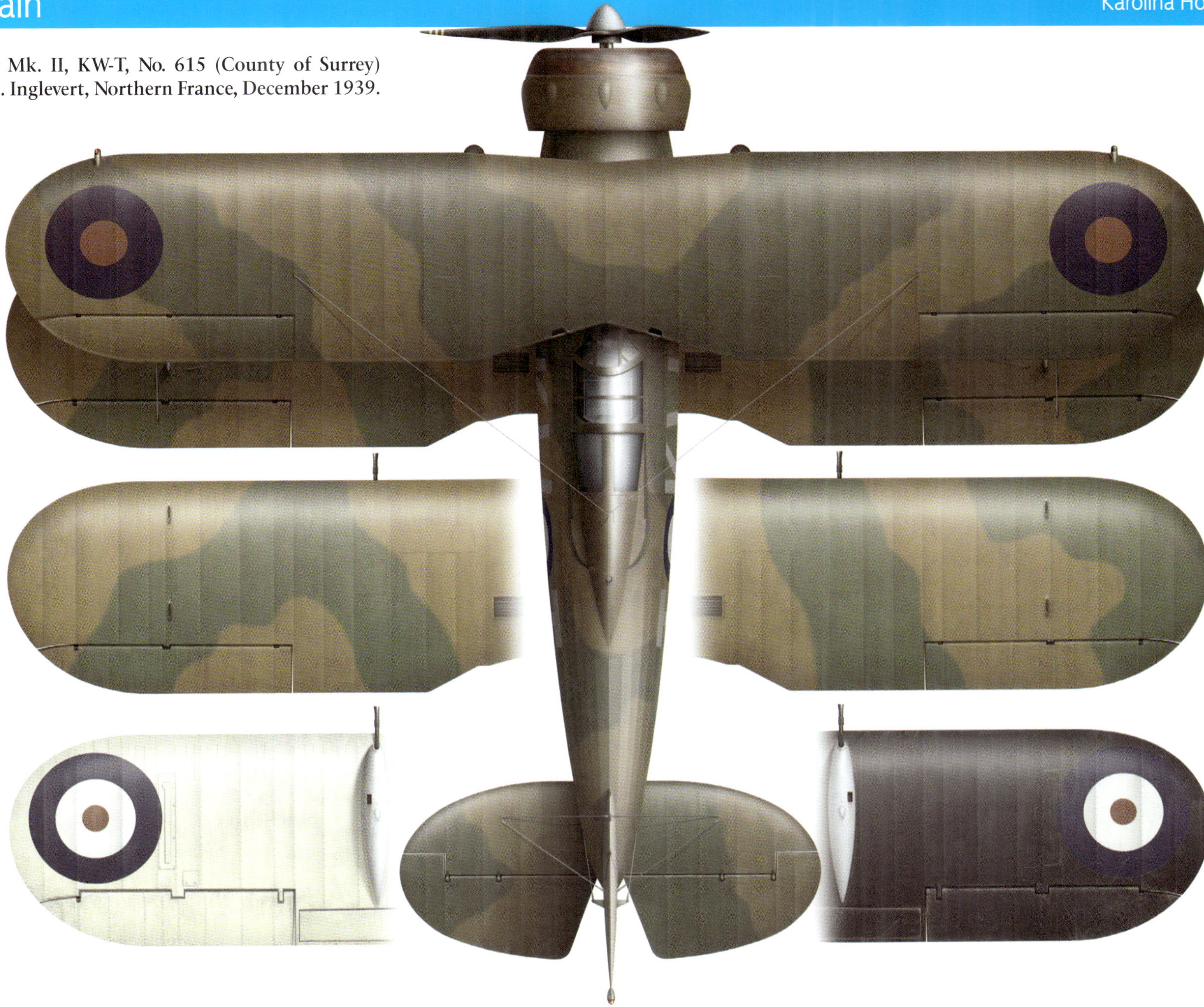

Gloster Gladiator Mk. I, LW-E, No. 607 Squadron, RAF, St. Inglevert, Northern France, 1939.

- Dark Green, Dark Earth – uppersurfaces with Day Night undersurface.

Gloster Gladiator Mk. I, serial K7995, LW-D, No. 607 Squadron, RAF, pilot Flt. Lt. John Sample, St. Inglevert, Northern France, 1939.

- Dark Green, Dark Earth – uppersurfaces with Day Night undersurface.

Gloster Gladiator Mk. I, LW-E, No. 607 Squadron, RAF,
St. Inglevert, Northern France, 1939.

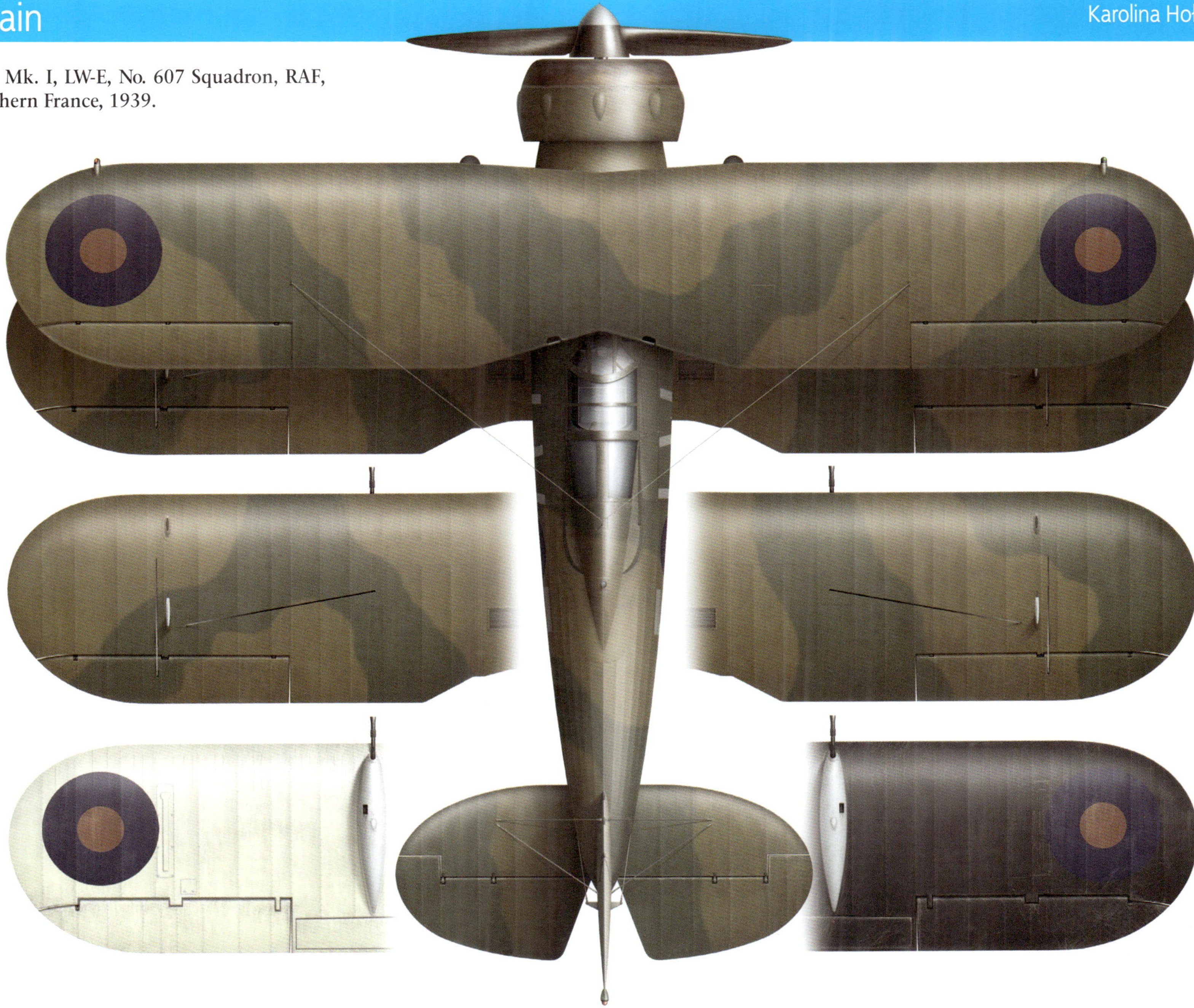

Artur Juszczak

Messerschmitt Bf 109E-1, 'Black 4' of 2./JG 27, pilot Fritz Keller, France, 1940.

- RLM 02, RLM 71 – uppersurfaces with RLM 65 undersurface.

Messerschmitt Bf 109E-3, W. Nr. 1559, 'White 1' of 1./JG 1, pilot Hptm. Wilhelm Balthasar, France, June 1940.

- RLM 02, RLM 71 – uppersurfaces with RLM 65 undersurface.

Messerschmitt Bf 109E-1, W.nr. 5102, 'Kieki' of Stab I/JG 77, pilot Hans Karl Keitel, France, April 1940.

- RLM 02, RLM 71 – uppersurfaces with RLM 65 undersurface.

Messerschmitt Bf 109E-3/N, W.Nr. 779, 'White 3 + –' of 4./JG 26, pilot Fw. Wilhelm 'Willi' Roth, France, 1940.

- RLM 02, RLM 71 – uppersurfaces with RLM 65 undersurface.

Messerschmitt Bf 109E-3, 'White 2' of Stab I./JG 52, Charleville, France, May1940.

- RLM 02, RLM 71 – uppersurfaces with RLM 65 undersurface.

Messerschmitt Bf 109E-3, 'White 2' of Stab I./JG 52, Charleville, France, May1940.

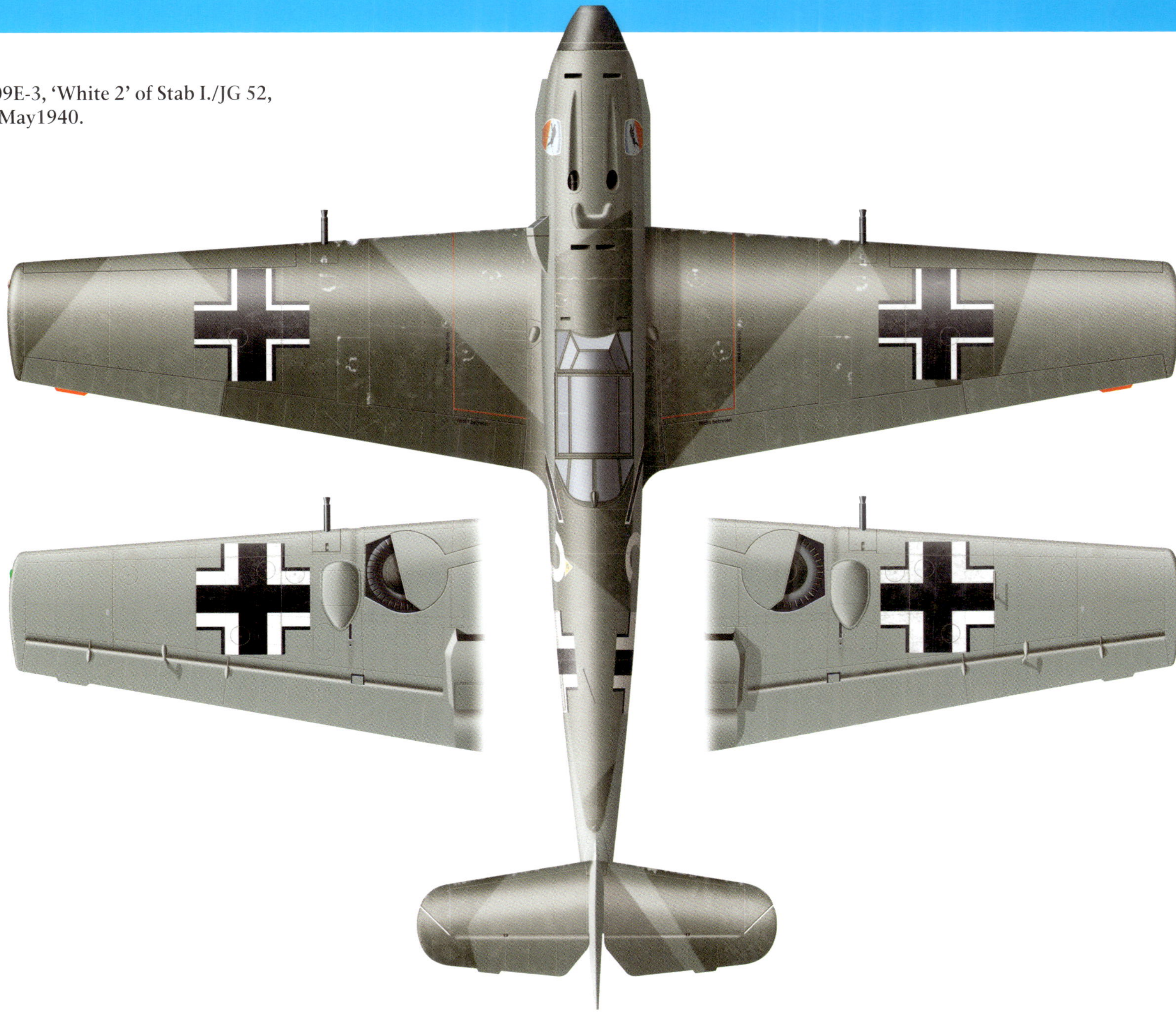

Messerschmitt Bf 109E-3, of III./JG 53, pilot Hptm. Werner Mölders, France, 25 May 1940.

- RLM 02 – uppersurfaces with RLM 65 undersurface.

Messerschmitt Bf 109E-3, of III./JG 53, pilot Hptm. Werner Mölders, France, 25 May 1940.

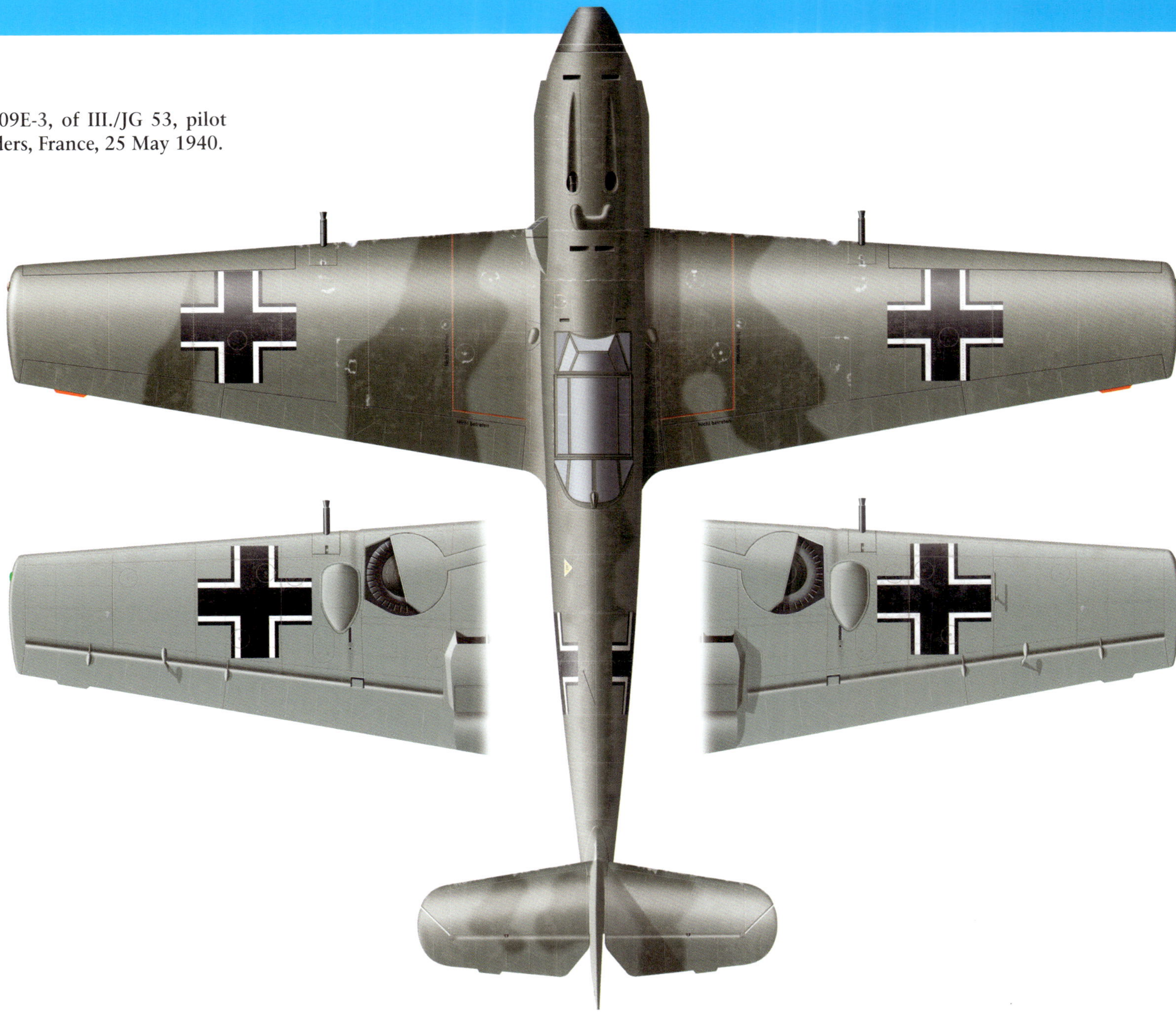

Messerschmitt Bf 109E-4, 'Yellow 1+~' of 9./JG 52. France, autumn 1940.

- *RLM 02, RLM 71 – uppersurfaces, fuselage sides heavily mottled with RLM 02/RLM71 with RLM 65 undersurface.*

Messerschmitt Bf 109E-3, W.Nr 936, or more probably W.Nr. 2764 of JG 26, pilot Adolf Galland, July France 1940.

- RLM 02, RLM 71 – uppersurfaces with RLM 65 undersurface.

Messerschmitt Bf 109E-3, W.Nr. 2161, J-313 of Swiss Flieger Kompagnie FlKp21, 1940.

- RLM 70 – uppersurfaces with RLM 65 undersurface.

Bf 108B, NM+NR of II./JG 53, Charleville, France, May 1940.

- RLM 63 overall with black nose.

Karolina Hołda

Messerschmitt Bf 110C-1, L1+IH of 1.(Z)/LG 1. France, May 1940. Aircraft was usually flown by Feldwebel Herbert Schob.

- RLM 70, RLM 71 – uppersurfaces, with RLM 65 undersurface.

Messerschmitt Bf 110C-1, 2N+GB of I./ZG 1. France, April 1940. Personal aircraft of Gruppenkomandeur Wolfgang Falck.

- RLM 70, RLM 71 – uppersurfaces, with RLM 65 undersurface.

Messerschmitt Bf 110C-1, 2N+CH, "Ilse" of 1./ZG 1. France, May 1940.

- RLM 70, RLM 71 – uppersurfaces, with RLM 65 undersurface. Individual letter "C", in white, were repeated on the upper wings oywards of the crosses.

Messerschmitt Bf 110C, W.Nr. 2831, 2N+GH of 5./ZG 1. France, June 1940. Personal aircraft of Manfred Dahne.

- RLM 70, RLM 71 – uppersurfaces, with RLM 65 undersurface.

Messerschmitt Bf 110C-4, L1+IH of 1./ZG 2. France, May 1940.

- RLM 70, RLM 71 – uppersurfaces, with RLM 65 undersurface.

Messerschmitt Bf 110C, M8+GN of 5./ZG 76. France, May 1940.

- RLM 70, RLM 71 – uppersurfaces, with RLM 65 undersurface.

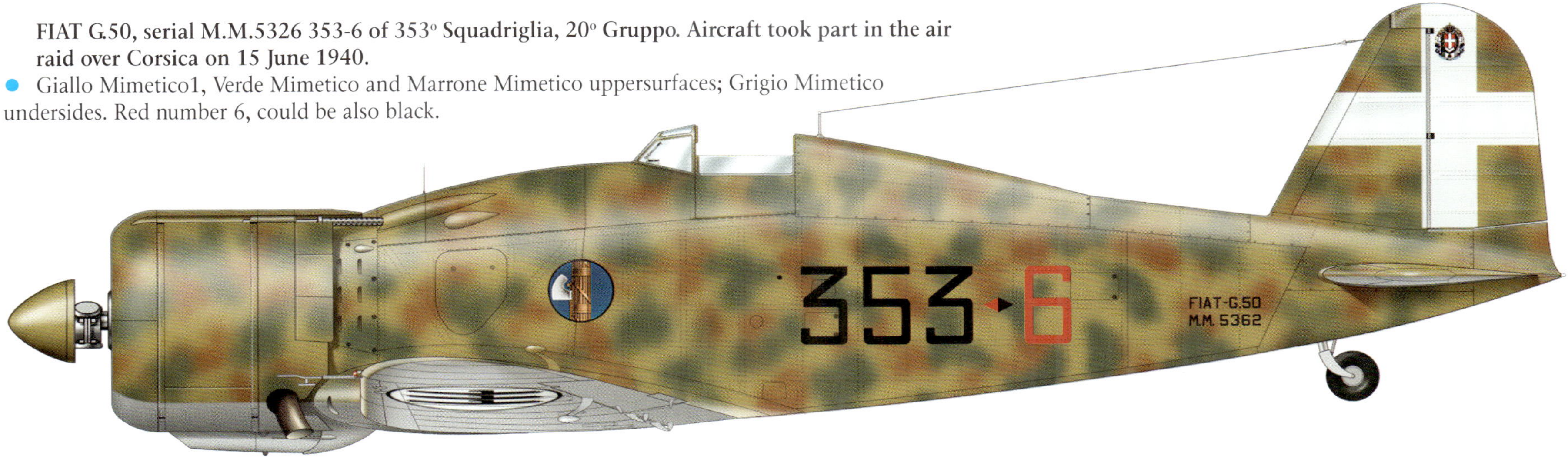

FIAT G.50, serial M.M.5326 353-6 of 353° Squadriglia, 20° Gruppo. Aircraft took part in the air raid over Corsica on 15 June 1940.

- Giallo Mimetico1, Verde Mimetico and Marrone Mimetico uppersurfaces; Grigio Mimetico undersides. Red number 6, could be also black.

FIAT CR.42, M.M.4462, 95-1 of 95° Squadriglia. Aircraft flown by Maggiore Ferruccio Vossilla, Commander of the 18° Gruppo, 56° Stormo, Novi Ligure, June 1940. The 18° Gruppo escorted BR.20 bombers during a raid over Toulon on 15th June 1940, where they were engaged by French MB.151 fighters.

- Giallo Mimetico, Verde Mimetico and Marrone Mimetico, upper sufaces with Aluminio undersides. Interplane struts in Grigio Azzurro Chiaro.

Richard J. Caruana

FIAT CR.42, M.M.4361, 71-1, of 75° Squadriglia, 23° Gruppo. Flown by Capt. Luigi Filippi, June 1940. He was taken prisoner on 15 June 1940, probably shot down by Adjudant-Chef Le Gloan of GC III/6 over Le Luc.

- Giallo Mimetico, Verde Mimetico and Marrone Mimetico upper surfaces with Aluminio undersides.

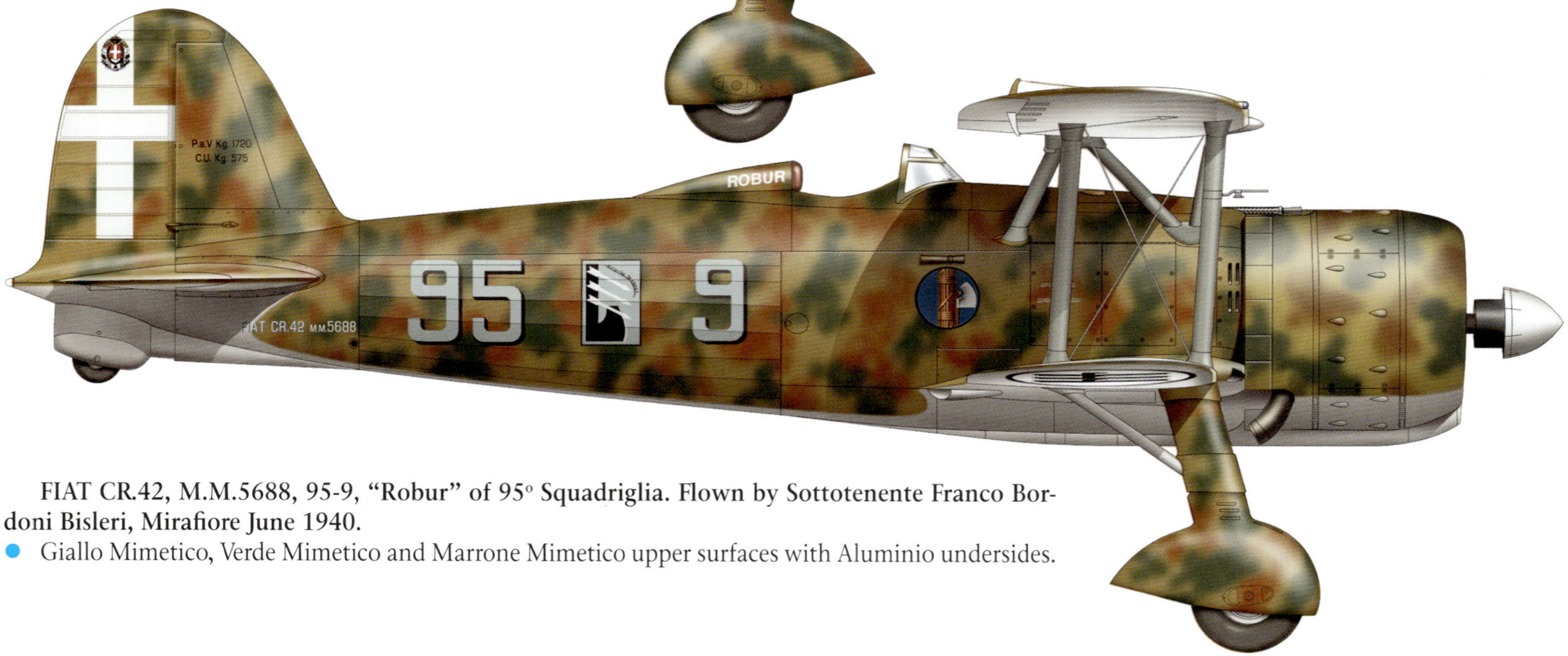

FIAT CR.42, M.M.5688, 95-9, "Robur" of 95° Squadriglia. Flown by Sottotenente Franco Bordoni Bisleri, Mirafiore June 1940.

- Giallo Mimetico, Verde Mimetico and Marrone Mimetico upper surfaces with Aluminio undersides.

Colour Chips

French Colours

Kaki mat (Vert Foncé mat)
FS 34098

Brun mat (Brun Foncé mat)
FS 30108

Gris Bleu Foncé mat
FS 36173

Gris Bleu Clair mat
FS 35237

British Colours

Dark Green
FS 34079

Light Green
FS 34172

Dark Earth
FS 30118

Light Earth
FS 30257

Night Black
FS 37038

White
FS 37778

German Colours

RLM 02
FS 34159

RLM 71
FS 34083

RLM 70
FS 34052

RLM 65
FS 35352

RLM 63
FS 36375

Italian Colours

Giallo Mimetico
FS 30266

Verde Mimetico
FS 34102

Marrone Mimetico
FS 30219

Alluminio
FS 17178

Grigio Azzurro Chiaro
FS 36307

Grigio Mimetico
FS 36293

Höchstgeschwindigkeit
mit voll ausgefahrenen
Landklappen 250 km/h
Netz-
Ausschalter
Achtung
Vor Anlassen
Farwerksschalter
auf „Ruhe"
Staurohr
Luftschraube
Handpumpe
Fahrgestell
EIN
EIN
Anzeige
AUS
AUS
Restland
Warnlampe
Liter
Ein
Aus
Fahrwerk
Griff ziehen
wenn Schalter
nicht zurückspringt
Notzug für Fahrwerk
Aus
Ein
Aus
Autholen
Aus
Betrieb

1. Altimeter (Fein-Groβhöhenmesser, Fl 22320);
2. Master compass (Führerkompass, Fl 23211);
3. Receptacle for Revi C/12D (Steckdose für REVI, Fl 32624);
4. Boost gauge (Ladedruckmesser, Fl 20550);
5. Compass deviation table (Deviationstabelle);
6. Airspeed indicator (Fahrtmesser, Fl 22231);
7. Turn and bank indicator (Wendezeiger, Fl 22402 mit Ventil, Fl 22403);
8. The propeller selection switch is located here in early versions (Verstellschalter für Luftschraube, Fl 18502);
9. Tachometer (Drehzahlmesser, Fl 20222-3);
10. Propeller pitch indicator (Stellungsanzeiger für Luftschraube, Fl 18503-2);
11. Ignition switch for magnetos panel (Zündschalter, Fl 21121-2);
12. Engine starter switch (Netzausschalter, Fl 32315-2);
13. Pitot head heating warning lamp (Gitterschauzeichen für Staurohrheizung, Fl 32525-3);
14. Radio selector panel (Schaltkasten für FT Fl 26858-1);
15. Machine guns rounds indicator (Schalt- und Kontrollkasten SKK 224, Fl 47293)
16. Cockpit lamp dimmer switch (Verdunkler, Fl 32401-2);
17. Blind panel (Blindplatte);
18. Doubled fuel and oil pressure gauge (Doppeldruckmesser, Fl 20512-2);
19. Undercarriage position indicator (Fahrwerksanzeige -Vierlampengerä, Fl 32526);
20. Undercarriage control lever (Fahrwerksanzeige -Vierlampengerät, Fl 32526);
21. Filter pump control lever (Handpumpenhebel für Kraftstoff-Filterpumpe);
22. Mechanical undercarriage position indicator (Fahrwerksanzeiger mechanisch Nr. 8-109.20-2201)
23. Main switch (Nullschussknopf, Fl 32302)
24. Fuel contents gauge (Vorratsanzeiger für Kraftstoff, Fl 20723);
25. Fuel lack warning lamp (Reststandswarnlampe Fl 32262-1);
26. Oil temperature gauge (Öltemperaturanzeiger Fl 20343);
27. Coolant temperature gauge (Kühlstofftemperaturanzeiger, Fl 20342-2);
28. Undercarriage emergency control lever
29. Instructions for flap settings, landing speed, etc
30. Board clock

Caudron-Renault CR.714 Cyclone Instrument Panel

Dariusz Karnas

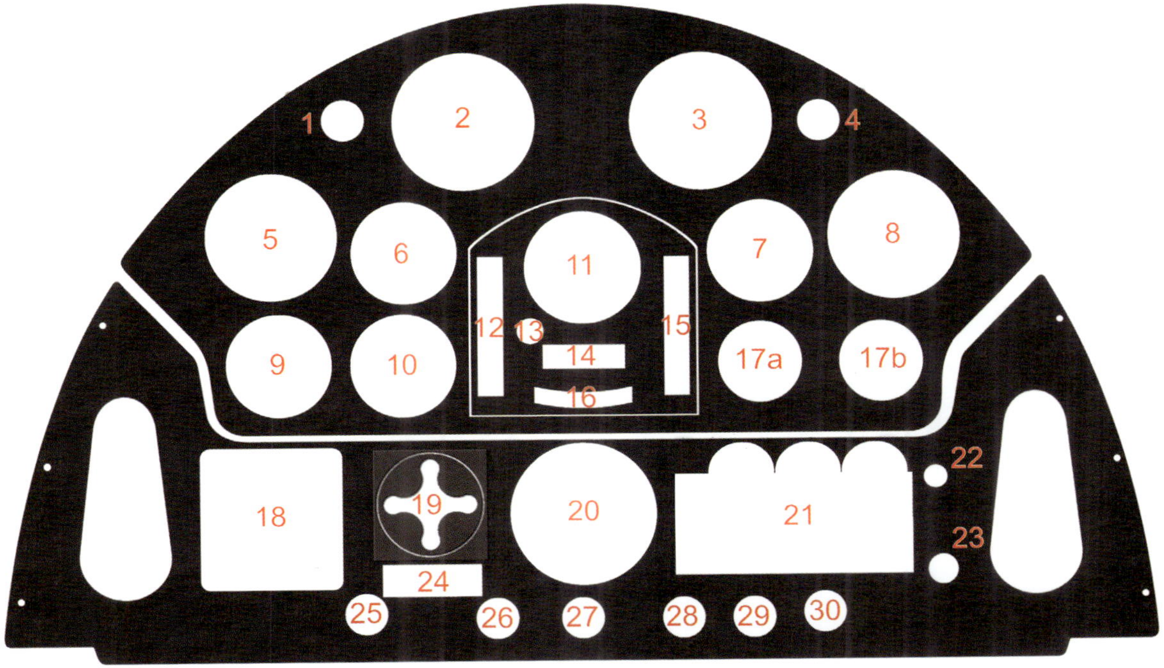

1. Tachometer switch
2. Landing speed indicator 60–200 km/h
3. Boost-manifold pressure indicator
4. End of camera gun film warning lamp
5. Tachometer
6. Fuel pressure indicator
7. Fuel indicator
8. Altimeter
9. Oil temperature indicator
10. Oil pressure indicator

Badin ACDFK type 54 D 120-700 km/h flight controller [11–16]:

11. 120–700 km/h airspeed indicator
12. Vertical speed indicator
13. Turn indicator adjustment knob
14. Turn indicator
15. Fore-and-aft level
16. Bank indicator

17a & b. Impar type P Modele 1937 ammunition counters

18. Ratier 106120 propeller control panel
19. VL 3534A undercarriage indicator
20. Aera type E10 compass
21. Messier armament selector
22. Pitot heating indicator lamp (green in original)
23. Pitot heating switch
24. Labinal 3587A undercarriage retraction indicator
25. Throttle limiter pull
26. Starter pull
27. Fire extinguisher pull
28. Main fuel valve pull
29. Carburettor heating pull
30. Fuel cut-off valve pull
31. Jaeger ignition switch
32. Lip 8-day clock
33. Messier 0-40 kg undercarriage hydraulic system pressure indicator
34. Messier 0-150 hpz (bar) undercarriage hydraulic system pressure indicator
35. Air-Equipement 0-50 hpz (bar) pneumatic system pressure indicator.

Hawker Hurricane Mk I Instrument Panel

Dariusz Karnas

Hawker Hurricane Mk I Instrument Panel

1. Airspeed indicator;
2. Artificial horizon;
3. Rate of climb indicator (Variometer);
4. Altimeter;
5. Direction indicator;
6. Adjusting knob for direction indicator;
7. Turning indicator;
8. Change over switch for undercarriage position visual indicator;
9. Undercarriage position visual indicator;
10. Compass correction card holder;
11. Oxygen flow indicator;
12. Oxygen supply indicator;
13. Oxygen regulator control valve;
14. Automatic boost cut-out control;
15. Engine starter push button;
16. Booster coil push button;
17. Main magneto switches;
18. Instrument switches;
pressure head heater switch;
navigation lamps switch;
cine camera switch;
19. Tachometer;
20. Reflector sight lamp switch;
21. Boost pressure gauge;
22. Fuel contents gauge selector switch;
23. Oil pressure gauge;
24. Fuel pressure gauge;
25. Fuel contents gauge;
26. Oil temperature gauge;
27. Radiator temperature gauge;
28. Starting magneto switch.

Dariusz Karnas

Curtiss H-75 Hawk Instrument Panel, metric instruments

Published in Poland in 2025
by STRATUS s.j.
ul. Żeromskiego 6A,
27-600 Sandomierz, Poland
e-mail: office@mmpbooks.biz
as
MMPBooks,
e-mail: rogerw@mmpbooks.biz

http://www.mmpbooks.biz

ISBN
978-83-67227-99-5

Editor in chief
Roger Wallsgrove

Editorial Team
Robert Pęczkowski
Artur Juszczak

Colour drawings
Richard J. Caruana
Karolina Hołda
Artur Juszczak
Dariusz Karnas
Teodor Liviu Moroşanu
Sławomir Zajączkowski

DTP
Wydawnictwo Stratus sp. j.

Printed by
Wydawnictwo Diecezjalne i Drukarnia
www.wds.pl

PRINTED IN POLAND